Praise for *Influence at Work*

"Readable, invaluable and based on the evidence. You can't ask for a better guide to influence than Steve Martin."

—Tim Harford, presenter of BBC Radio 4's *More or Less* and host of the *Cautionary Tales* podcast

"With his characteristic rigour and clarity, Steve Martin presents a practical and powerful framework for persuasion. This book is an essential read for leaders, managers and anyone who wants to increase their impact at work."

—Daniel H. Pink, *New York Times* no. 1 bestselling author of *To Sell Is Human* and *The Power of Regret*

"Outstanding. The best account I have seen of how to acquire and employ the highly desirable prize of influence. Engagingly written, evidence-based and ethically sound. This book is superb."

—Robert B. Cialdini, bestselling author of *Influence: The Psychology of Persuasion*

"A modern-day manifesto for an age-old and crucial skill. Practical, immediately usable tools to boost your influence without sacrificing your integrity."

—James Timpson, CEO of Timpson's and *Sunday Times* columnist

"A clever, entertaining jaunt through the unspoken rules which govern influence at work."

—Camilla Cavendish, *Financial Times*

"Eminently practical and evidence-based, this terrific guide will help you wield more influence at work and beyond."

—Katy L. Milkman, professor at the Wharton School and bestselling author of *How to Change*

"An absorbing, credible and applicable guide for anyone interested in successfully persuading others. Which is all of us."
—Senator John Barrasso MD, United States Congress

"Steve Martin reveals the underlying formula of that most elusive of skills, influence. An extremely practical guide full of precise, actionable steps that anyone can take to become more influential at work."
—Vanessa Bohns, Professor of Organizational Behavior, Cornell University, and author of *You Have More Influence Than You Think*

"A comprehensive map for navigating the modern workplace. Clear and evidenced, the book should be required reading for any practising leader."
—Alex Aiken, Executive Director, UK Government Communications

"I love this book. It provokes curiosity every time I pick it up. Steve has a wonderful way of helping you understand how to influence through clear, principle-based thinking. An outstanding resource that I recommend for any leader."
—John "Mitch" Mitchell, England Head Coach, Rugby Football Union

"Written with skill and humour, this accessible and practical book shows how all of us can gain more influence at work and in our personal lives too."
—Stephan Meier, James P. Gorman Professor of Business at Columbia Business School and author of *The Employee Advantage*

"A great read. Practical, to-the-point advice for anyone who needs to boost their influence."
—Dil Sidhu, Head of Birkbeck Business School, University of London

Influence at Work

Influence at Work

Capture attention, connect with others,
convince people to act

Steve J. Martin

INFLUENCE AT WORK

Published with permission from *The Economist* by Pegasus Books.

The Economist is an imprint of
Pegasus Books, Ltd.
148 West 37th Street, 13th Floor
New York, NY 10018

First Pegasus Books cloth edition September 2024

ISBN: 978-1-63936-714-6

10 9 8 7 6 5 4 3 2 1

Printed in the United States of America
Distributed by Simon & Schuster
www.pegasusbooks.com

PEGASUS BOOKS
NEW YORK LONDON

To Bob.

And to Linds.

About the author

Steve J. Martin is a Royal Society nominated author in the field of influence and persuasion science and CEO of Influence at Work (UK). He is co-author of several bestselling books including *Messengers: Who We Listen To, Who We Don't and Why* and the *New York Times, Wall Street Journal* and *Business Week* bestseller, *Yes! 50 Secrets from the Science of Persuasion.* His books have sold over 1.75 million copies and have been translated into 27 languages.

A highly sought-after adviser to leaders in business and policy, Steve's work in the psychology of influence and persuasion has featured in the academic, business and international press including *Nature*, the *New York Times*, BBC TV and radio, *The Times, Washington Post, Financial Times, Harvard Business Review* and *Time* magazine.

Steve is Faculty Director of Behavioural Science (Exec. Ed.) at Columbia Business School and has been a guest lecturer on MBA and Senior Executive programmes at London Business School, Harvard and the London School of Economics.

He lives in London.

Also in the Economist Edge series

Branding That Means Business
by Matt Johnson and Tessa Misiaszek

Innovating with Impact
by Ted Ladd and Alessandro Lanteri

Giving Good Feedback
by Margaret Cheng

Best Story Wins: Storytelling for business success
by Mark Edwards

Contents

Introduction

"What am I doing wrong?" asked Sam, looking up at her friends, her expression a mix of frustration and fatigue.

Everything had been going so well. Despite being in her job for almost three years, her delight at being offered a dream role with a well-positioned company in the city had never faded. It had been a busy time. And a successful one. Pushing any insecurities she felt to the back of her mind, Sam had committed to grasping every opportunity that came her way. As a result, she had captured the attention of several managers in the firm who seemed happy to champion her enthusiasm, work ethic and attention to detail. Within a year she landed a promotion. Shortly after her second anniversary she stepped up again. This time as a manager herself, a role she was assured would offer more responsibility and influence. But as she reflected in the company of friends, she realised that only the first of these turned out to be true.

More responsibility? Certainly. Sam had never been busier.

But influence? Not so much.

A case in point was a meeting that had taken place earlier in the week. As part of her responsibilities, Sam attended the quarterly resources meeting. The gathering required a dozen or so junior managers to deliver updates on people and projects to the company's directors and, in doing so, make their pitch for the resources needed for the next three months. Sam had been told how important it was to prepare for these meetings, which would routinely descend into a bunfight. The latest meeting was no exception. Despite her meticulously prepared spreadsheets and thoughtful contingency plans, she found herself losing out again to others whose appeals for extra resources were certainly no better than her own. Some were considerably worse.

"Tell me about it," grumbled Jake, who was sitting at the table listening. "I've been at my place for almost five years. Nothing ever changes. We're told that to get anything signed off we need to focus on the two essentials: facts and finances. So that's what I do. Yet I can count on the fingers of one hand the number of times that people listen. You'd think the bosses of a data analytics company might actually use data to inform their decisions. But no. We're told what we need to do to influence the decision-making, but the reality is very different."

*

Sam and Jake's situations are very common. Every day we face the challenge of influencing and persuading others at work. Sometimes the people we need to persuade are higher up the organisational food chain: bosses, managers and senior decision-makers. At other times they are our peers. Sometimes they are team members who report to us. Often, they're not colleagues at all but customers, clients, constituents or patients.

Regardless of who they are, the odds of us accomplishing our goals and objectives will frequently be determined by our ability to influence and persuade them. But skills like influence and persuasion are not straightforward. We might like to believe that appeals and requests based on the best evidence and backed up by the right economic arguments win the day, but the reality is often different. In today's competitive, fast-moving and attention-scarce world, having a good case to make is simply not enough. Because, as Sam, Jake and millions of others like them are realising, having a good case to make is not the same as making your case well.

To be successful at work you have to be influential at work, which requires an understanding of how the rules of influence work. Not just those dictated by logic, finance and company policy but also the unspoken rules. The rules people rarely talk about, but that frequently have an outsized impact on who and what is listened to and done; and who and what is ignored. Understanding and navigating these rules of influence is crucial to your persuasive success.

I'm often asked whether some people are simply born with these skills. Are they members of a lucky group who have the instinctive ability to persuade others? Although it may be true that some people are naturally blessed with more than their fair share of persuasive powers, that certainly doesn't mean that the rest of us will never be able to compete, for an important reason. Influence is a skill that can be learned and mastered. No one need resign themselves to looking on enviously as others achieve their goals and objectives while their own languish. Anyone can become a more successful and accomplished influencer and this straight-talking, practical book will show you how.

This is a book about how to make your case well.

Although this book focuses primarily on improving your ability to influence people at work, the lessons and insights are equally applicable in your personal life. Crucially, it will help you to become an effective persuader without compromising your ethics, your values, or feeling as if you're being manipulative.

*

This book is divided into three parts, each comprising three chapters. In Chapter 1 you will get the chance to assess how influential you are currently. The short test will provide you with feedback on the approaches you most commonly rely on when attempting to persuade others at work. You don't have to complete the test to read the rest of the book and you can skip straight to the beginning of Chapter 2 if you prefer. But I recommend you complete the test because it will provide a potentially helpful and personalised benchmark to track your progress as you develop your skills and knowledge.

Chapter 2 explores the history of influence and defines what it actually is. This is important because the term "influence" is frequently used interchangeably (and even confused) with other concepts like persuasion, power, compliance, negotiation, campaigning and selling. Although there are parallels and similarities, influence is arguably more important because it lies at the heart of any meaningful change.

Chapter 3 busts some of the common myths and misperceptions about the influence process. Much of the received wisdom about how to influence others is often more fiction than fact. This book provides you with the facts. In addition to exploring the fundamental human motivations at the heart of why people do what they do, Chapter 3 also introduces you to the Influence Equation. Consider it a formula of sorts, which anyone can use to become a more successful influencer. The Influence Equation shows how anyone can create a successful influence strategy based on the optimal combination of evidence, economics and emotions; with the amount of each depending on the context of the situation you face. Put another way, successful influence is about building and communicating your case based on the right mix of facts, finance and feelings.

Part 2 dives deeper into the three components of the Influence Equation, devoting a chapter to each. Chapter 4 explores how successful influence is frequently achieved not necessarily by the volume and quality of evidence presented but by the way certain evidence is presented. I will show how the person who delivers a message is often more important than its truth and how stories often supplant statistics in the minds of those we want to persuade.

Chapter 5 focuses on how to influence people using economic and financial arguments. I will show that people's reactions to incentives are often shaped by psychological mechanisms rather than rational computation. Don't get me wrong; I am not dismissive of incentives. They can be a wonderful tool for influence – universally loved, widely understood and easy to implement. But that doesn't make them universally successful. I will outline some of the upsides and downsides of using economic incentives to persuade others and suggest how best to deploy them.

Chapter 6 explores the role that emotions play in successful influence strategies. Many people claim that all decisions are triggered by some emotional element or component. It is a perspective I tend to agree with. The chapter describes specific emotions that can have a particularly powerful and persuasive effect on people, along with suggestions on how to use them in effective and ethical ways.

Part 3 is all about the principles, the practice and the ethics of influence. Chapter 7 reviews seven universal principles of influence founded on the work of the eminent social psychologist Robert Cialdini, with whom I am lucky to have trained and worked for more than two decades. In Chapter 8 I turn to the practice of influence by reviewing some of the common challenges that people face at work. Although most of us believe our influence challenges are unique, in reality many of the challenges we face when persuading others are similar. Chapter 8 offers practical, actionable approaches and strategies for a range of common influence scenarios with suggestions about how they can be tailored to your own context and circumstances. Chapter 9 wraps up by exploring an important aspect of modern-day influence: its ethics. Just because we can influence others doesn't mean we always should. The book ends with a checklist that you might find helpful to create influence strategies that are effective yet do not compromise your values or integrity.

In today's workplace of flatter structures, virtual working and cross-cultural collaboration, where coercion is reviled, playing the "I'm the boss" card can cost you dearly and sucking up "sucks", there is one skill more than any other that is critical to your success: the ability to navigate the rules of successful influence at work.

In the following pages I will show you these rules and also how to employ them effectively and ethically to command attention, connect with others, win over the sceptics, sway the undecided, unify the polarised and motivate people to act.

PART 1

Influence: what it is and why it's important

Overview

LinkedIn – a social media platform owned by Microsoft and primarily used by professionals to network, share ideas and find jobs – frequently conducts surveys to keep abreast of workplace trends, the interests of employers and the changing views of workers. Given that millions use the platform to share unbridled views of their bosses' shortcomings, colourful accounts of co-workers' oddities and updates on the "state of work", it can be considered a useful barometer of the current attitudes and perspectives in offices and factories around the world.

One survey asks a straightforward question: "What are the most important and desirable skills that employees should possess?" Dynamic markets require a dizzying range of changing skills and smarts, so answers vary over time. Context matters too. Certain industries and jobs require skills that others have no use for. The ability to ensure that a balance sheet balances is a useful skill for financiers but not so much for firefighters. Yet one skill appears ubiquitous to employers' wish lists, regardless of the job or where in the world it is located.

Influence.

Surveys like these illustrate the vital role that influence plays in the workplace and in life more generally. They show why the demand for people who possess the skills and abilities to convince and motivate others has been a near constant since the dawn of humankind. Influence is rather like a secret sauce.

9

Without influence it's hard to make progress and effect change. Influence can transform an otherwise routine idea or easily ignored message into a compelling vision that opens minds and doors, turns doubters into supporters and intentions into actions.

But influence is also frequently misunderstood. Over the next three chapters I will explore what influence is and, importantly, what it isn't. I will review some of the received wisdoms about how to connect with, convince and change the actions and minds of others and, in doing so, question how reliable they really are. I will highlight some of the common myths and misperceptions about how the influence process works. And I will provide an approach, in the form of the Influence Equation, that any inspiring influencer can use to create powerful and persuasive influence strategies.

To begin with, though, I want to give you the chance to assess your current and preferred approach to persuading others.

1

Your influence, at work

This short test will help you assess your current approach to influencing others and demonstrate where and how you could improve your skills. Although primarily designed for workplace situations, the insights could be useful when influencing people in your personal life too. It should take no more than 15 minutes to complete and is entirely optional. If you would prefer to get straight into the book, skip directly to Chapter 2.

If you would like to take the test online you can follow the QR code below or visit influenceatwork.co.uk/the_economist. And if you are a manager or leader of people, you are free to share the QR code with your teams so they can take the test too (it's completely free).

How the test works

In this test you will be presented with 10 influence challenges, each with three possible approaches to dealing with the situation. Consider each challenge in turn and distribute a total of 10 points across the three suggested approaches in a way that best represents how you would act if you were facing this situation in real life.

For example, if you feel that one of the responses is completely aligned with how you would act, assign all ten points to that scenario and zero points to the remaining two responses. However, if you are wavering about how you would react, distribute the ten points across the responses in a way that best reflects your point of view. For example, you might assign six points to the approach you are leaning most towards, three points to your second-choice answer and one point to the approach you are least convinced about. You can distribute the ten points across all three responses, or to just one or two, but it is important that the points you distribute for each scenario always add up to ten.

There are no right or wrong answers.

The 10 influence challenges

1. At the last minute your manager has asked you to prepare a presentation for an important meeting she is attending tomorrow. As you are working on another project that also needs finishing today, you need to ask one of your colleagues for help. You have a reasonably good working relationship with this colleague but wouldn't consider them a friend. What would your approach be?

Use the boxes alongside the three suggested approaches to distribute a total of 10 points in a way that best represents how you would act.

a.	Ask your colleague to prepare the whole presentation. If they say no, ask them if they could at least contribute in some way, perhaps by reviewing some of the data you have collected.	
b.	Before asking for their help, explain what has happened and promise that if the situation was ever reversed, you would obviously be more than happy to help them.	
c.	Offer to take them to the pub for drinks on you in exchange for their help.	

2. You have been tasked with crafting an email designed to persuade your colleagues to attend a training course. Attendance at previous training events have been notoriously low. What approach would you take to increase attendance?

a.	Highlight the fact that there are limited places on the course and the next course may not be for several months.	
b.	List three clear reasons why people should attend at the top of your email invite.	
c.	Tell a compelling story about how a lesson you gained from the previous company training event has had a huge impact on you.	

3. A new piece of software has been made available that will increase the efficiency and quality of your team's output. But resources are tight and your department's budgets have been pared back considerably. How would you persuade your boss to prioritise your need for the new software over the appeals of your colleagues who are also pitching for funds?

a.	Demonstrate the future savings that the company will lose out on if you do not get the software.	
b.	Produce a set of slides summarising your proposal, supported by financial facts, figures and a benefit analysis.	
c.	Enthusiastically paint a picture of how your boss will benefit, by describing how everyone using the new software will be so much more efficient in the future.	

4. Your company has been slow to adopt some of the environmental practices being promoted in the office such as recycling, sharing rides to work, reducing the use of paper, and turning off lights and appliances when not in use. How would you persuade more of your colleagues to embrace sustainable initiatives and act on them every day?

a.	Introduce a competition between departments where those with the lowest annual energy consumption are rewarded with an extra day's holiday.	
b.	Display provocative pictures around the office on the impact of climate change (e.g. sad-looking polar bears on melting ice caps), with a request that people "conserve energy for the sake of the environment".	
c.	Clearly communicate the obvious advantages of the energy-saving measures being advocated, like saving the company money.	

5. Your department has identified a way to make a significant efficiency at work and you are keen to trial the idea. But employees are becoming fatigued with the sheer volume of initiatives and are often resistant to new ideas. What approach would you to take to open their minds?

a. Present everyone with two options: one requiring much more effort and harder to implement, and a second, more realistic idea. The hope is that most people accept the easier, more attractive second option.	
b. Ask teams to calculate how much time they are currently wasting by not embracing this new approach. Then ask them what they would do with the additional time created by the initiative you are proposing.	
c. Be up front and honest. Admit there have been a lot of previous initiatives that probably haven't worked but passionately express how if your department keeps doing things the "old way", it will never grow and prosper.	

6. You and your team are leading a project that desperately needs additional resources. But other departments are also competing for limited resources. How will you persuade the decision-makers to prioritise your project when they allocate resources?

a. Conduct a thorough analysis of the various projects that need extra resources and then ask someone who you know is close to the budget-holder to speak on your behalf.	
b. Describe the negative impact of your project being under-resourced by comparing your situation with "a football team that has six players for an 11-a-side game" – a match they are sure to lose.	
c. Demonstrate how your project serves a joint purpose that helps other departments. Make the point that starving your project of resources will result in many other projects being at risk of failure.	

7. You excel in your role and believe you deserve a pay rise. How do you persuade your manager that the value you provide to the company is worth a salary increase?

a.	Be empathetic. Acknowledge how annoying it must be for your manager to have people coming to them all the time asking to be paid more. Say that you are struggling and, given your good work record, you believe your request is reasonable and fair.	
b.	Be bold. Say you have heard that some of the company's competitors are offering 15% raises to some of their staff, but you'd be very happy with 10%.	
c.	Get your timing right. Wait until the beginning of the new budget year, so your request is a much smaller proportion of what's in the overall pot than it is now.	

8. You and your colleagues are seeking to convince bosses that offering remote working on certain days will boost both productivity and work–life balance. How do you persuade them to adopt a more flexible approach?

a.	Book a series of face-to-face meetings with various managers to provide a human account of how productivity and staff well-being improves on the days that people work from home.	
b.	Prepare a presentation with data showing the relationship between productivity and well-being, pointing out the time and productivity lost through commuting.	
c.	You suspect your manager isn't convinced about home working, so enlist the help of one of his peers who not only supports home working but does it herself. Sometimes it's not what's said but who says it that matters.	

9. You have developed a new product, but early feedback suggests some customers are sceptical about its viability. How would you build a proposition that communicates the clear benefits of the product and also gains the buy-in of some of your sceptical but important prospective clients?

a.	Develop a programme to educate customers so they can come to an informed, rather than an intuitive, decision about it.	
b.	Do a deal with a smaller number of trusted clients who will trial the product and provide feedback, allowing you to adapt and co-create the final release together.	
c.	Draw a parallel between your product and a now-well-known and extremely successful product that was also subject to a great deal of scepticism during the early days of its release.	

10. Two members of your team have just had another heated disagreement, which is having a negative effect on the rest of the team. You need to mediate and persuade them to work together amicably. What approach do you take?

a.	Assign them both to an important, high-profile project that they must jointly lead and be responsible for delivering successfully. Inform them that a member of the executive team is a sponsor, implicitly suggesting they will look like fools to leadership if they fail to work together.	
b.	Get them to look beyond their disagreement and create a sense of connection. Arrange a meeting where, before discussing their differences, they identify a shared commonality before delving into the reasons for their dispute.	
c.	Play hard ball. Explicitly lay out the likely outcomes and sanctions they could face, including disciplinary action for them both, if they fail to manage their frustrations with each other.	

Scoring sheet

Once you have completed the test, transfer the points from each scenario to the scoring sheet. Please pay careful attention and note that the order of the responses is not the same in every row. Once you have completed the scoring sheet, add up and complete the total for each column. This will give you an overall score for evidence-based, economic-based and emotional-based influence approaches.

1	a		b		c	
2	b		c		a	
3	b		a		c	
4	c		b		a	
5	a		c		b	
6	a		b		c	
7	b		a		c	
8	c		a		b	
9	a		c		b	
10	c		b		a	
Totals	Evidence score		Emotions score		Economics score	

I scored highest on Evidence: the data aficionado

People who prefer to base their arguments on evidence are typically detail-oriented, ensuring they offer advice and build proposals based on a solid foundation of data and proof. They might spend time carrying out research and will be careful to gather data, facts, statistics and expert opinions when constructing a persuasion strategy. They ensure that their arguments are well structured and logically coherent, drawing on credible information to back up their assertions. They are more likely to value accuracy and precision when it comes to persuading others. Their desire to persuade people to change might sometimes result in them overwhelming people or becoming impatient when others are slow to connect the dots.

When it comes to influence at work, these are the people most likely to say: "It's all about the facts!"

I scored highest on Emotions: the empathetic orator

People who place emotional appeals at the heart of their arguments strive to persuade people by prioritising feelings over facts. They frequently empathise with their audiences, tailoring messages in a way that resonates on an emotional level and takes account of different perspectives. They create connections with others that foster trust and will often use anecdotes and analogies to make their arguments more relatable and powerful. They can be skilled at defusing tension, helping people to find common ground and promoting constructive dialogue. They are often creative and can think "on the fly". Some people might accuse them of being idealistic and may even question the practicality of their ideas.

When it comes to influence at work, these are the people most likely to say: "Focus on feelings!"

I scored highest on Economics: the calculating connoisseur

People who favour a pragmatic and rational approach to influencing and persuading others will often incorporate economic reason and incentives into their arguments. They will often evaluate the costs and benefits of various options and then make their appeal based on what people will stand to gain or lose economically. They like using financial incentives to influence others, believing that most people care mostly about money, costs and resources. Some people might view them rather like "a spreadsheet in human form".

When it comes to influence at work, these are the people most likely to say: "It's about the finance!"

*

The test you have just undertaken has not been designed to provide a definitive evaluation of who you are, or of your personality traits. There are much better tests designed specifically to do that and they are readily available should you wish to seek them out. This test should be viewed as a simple snapshot of your preferred style when it comes to influencing and persuading others. Consider it a starting point for learning more about the influence process and as a way to identify how you might hone and improve your skills.

In reality, the effective influencer leverages a combination of approaches appropriate to a specific context or situation, rather than relying on a single approach. The ability to influence and persuade others is not one-size-fits-all. It is much more dynamic and context-dependent, requiring agility, alertness and a willingness to experiment. It is also a skill founded on a set of robust principles that anyone can learn more about and apply. In the same way a skilled chef combines flavours in a dish, or a mixologist blends ingredients in a cocktail, the master of influence is successful by combining the optimal mix of evidence, economics and emotions into their appeals and arguments.

2
The history of influence

The first act

The history of influence is a long one. The desire to capture an audience's attention, convince the undecided and inspire people to change has been a near-constant since the dawn of humankind. Some of the earliest written records about how to influence others are not in the texts of Greek philosophers but in the works of the ancient Egyptians and Chinese. Ptahhotep was a city administrator and vizier (akin to a modern-day minister) during the fifth Egyptian dynasty. He wrote what is widely regarded as the world's oldest textbook. Titled *Maxims* and written in the early 24th century BC, Ptahhotep offered advice and wisdom on the betterment of society by encouraging citizens to establish a "cosmic order" and "social harmony". He wrote about the importance of good table manners, how to conduct oneself appropriately in social circles and how to reason with (or, better still, avoid) argumentative people.[1] At over 4,000 years old, it is probably the world's first recorded text on social influence.

Lao Tzu, a Chinese "Old Master", similarly wrote an ancient text providing insight and wisdom to citizens, which went on to influence the major schools of Chinese philosophy and religion. A mark of the book's impact is that it remains in print today.[2]

Although both books were designed primarily as manuals of wisdom and advice for citizens, it is interesting to note the contrast in approaches used to persuade their respective audiences. Ptahhotep wrote of the negative consequences should audiences not follow his advice, replete with tales of what citizens stood to lose if they failed to comply. Tzu's approach was much more positive, highlighting the advantages and benefits available to readers should they be persuaded by his lessons. It is a debate that remains as relevant today as it was centuries ago. When attempting to persuade others, should you focus on the positives that your audience will experience if they follow your proposal – or the negatives if they do not? Thousands of years later, it is a debate that rumbles on.

When looking back on the history of influence and persuasion, most attention falls on the instructive works of the Greek philosophers, notably Aristotle in the fourth century BC. Many of his musings about the persuasion process, like those of his Egyptian and Chinese forebears, are as relevant today as ever.

Aristotle was a pioneer. His work *Rhetoric*, although never intended for publication, remains one of the most important texts ever written on the process of persuasion. Aristotle conceived that there are three main routes to effective persuasion: logos, ethos and pathos.[3]

Logos refers to logic or reason. Aristotle argued that at the heart of any persuasive appeal is a point of view or claim held by the individual or group looking to make an impact. He referred to this kind of persuasion as probative – a legal term that places the burden on a speaker or proposer to offer proof or evidence that supports their case. Logos also provides a structure for creating a persuasive argument because it infers that there is a connection between what is being proposed and the facts and beliefs that the audience already hold. A health food company providing statistics in advertisements about the nutritional value of its products is an example of logos, especially to people who already see themselves as health-conscious consumers.

Aristotle's second route to persuasion, ethos, concerns not the commentary of the communicator but their character. Is the speaker credible? Do they appear trustworthy? Although Aristotle provides little in terms of the specifics of what makes a credible or trustworthy communicator, he offers a useful insight about when an individual or group is more likely to be persuaded by a messenger rather than their message: during times of uncertainty. "Although people follow the trustworthy speaker more quickly and easily than an untrusted one," he observed, "in affairs where options waver, they will especially be looked upon to decide the case." (Unlike Aristotle, this book has a lot to say about what makes a credible and trustworthy influencer, and these are addressed in later chapters.)

This is important. It suggests, and countless examples prove the case, that often it's not the message itself that carries sway, but rather a feature of the messenger that exerts a persuasive impact. It is a concept that lies at the core of why some people in society – certain online influencers, climate deniers and politicians – are listened to and gain influential notoriety regardless of the legitimacy of what they are spouting. It's not what they are saying that makes them influential (logos), but who they are perceived to be (ethos).

The third of Aristotle's routes of persuasion is pathos, referring to emotion. An individual or group, he observes, is influenced to the extent that the proposal they hear causes them to feel an emotion that either directly or indirectly affects their judgement. In one particularly far-sighted passage, Aristotle observes that a judge in a friendly mood is likely to see an offender's act in a different way to the same wrongdoer viewed through angry eyes. I say far-sighted for good reason. Millennia later, a 2009 review of more than 1,000 judgements made in a judicial system found the likelihood of a prison inmate being granted bail peaked at 65% at the start of the day, but fell to almost zero just before lunch.[4] Perhaps those running prisons prioritised prisoners who had the best behaviour records, and hence the best chances of parole, to appear before the court first? But this would not explain why bail rates rose back to 65% after lunch. And also after each break. A better explanation is Aristotle's pathos. It wasn't the merits (logos) of the individual case that carried sway, neither was it the perceived trustworthiness of the prisoner nor the credibility of the person representing them (ethos). It was the emotion (pathos) they were experiencing that was directly influencing their judgements. The judges were viewing the offenders through "hangry" eyes.

A couple of centuries later the Roman Empire also had a significant and lasting influence, but through more formal means. The Romans were the first to establish legal procedures and protocols which included trials by jury, civil rights laws, the writing of wills and even the incorporation of businesses and companies, all of which remain today. The Roman Empire was also responsible for another related modern-day phenomenon: the paid influencer.

Much is made of today's highly paid celebrities and sports stars augmenting their income by accepting vast sums from firms in exchange for advocating their clothing, cosmetics and smartphones. But these sums pale in comparison with the paid influencers of Roman times. In addition to a percentage of any winnings, the best gladiators were frequently offered inducements in exchange for promotions. One charioteer,

Gaius Appuleius Diocles, is reputed to be the highest paid athlete in history with many of his riches coming from paid endorsements. Over a 24-year career that ended in 146 AD, Diocles amassed close to 36 million sesterces (around $12 billion today) in prize money.[5]

Many of history's literary giants were also commentators and keen observers of the influence process. William Shakespeare typically viewed persuasion as a rather dark art. Consequently, it appears in many of his plays as a mechanism for scheming and subterfuge. In *All's Well That Ends Well*, the loutish and capricious Parolles encourages Bertram, the young Count, to exploit his position in the court by wooing those who "eat, speak, and move, under the influence of the most receiv'd star".[6] Interestingly, the literal meaning of Parolles is "words" – implying that he really was all talk and no conviction. Perhaps Parolles provided Shakespeare with the opportunity to provide would-be persuaders of the day with a lesson that remains just as valid today. Words will get you so far, but at a certain point they become meaningless unless accompanied by action.

Shakespeare was not alone in casting influence as a worrisome art. Oscar Wilde's 1891 novel *The Picture of Dorian Gray* also embraced an alarming view of its impact.[7] One of the book's central characters, Lord Henry, delights in using his wit and charisma to impress, influence and hoodwink others. Having convinced Dorian of numerous fascinating and indulgent yet ultimately wrong and poisonous theories, he appears joyous as he professes: "All influence is immoral."

"Because to influence a person", he adds, "is to give him one's own soul."

The second act: from art to science, dark to light

For a significant amount of humankind's existence, influence has typically been viewed as an art form of sorts, frequently a dark one. A God-given skill afforded to a privileged few to exert, exploit and effect its power over those less fortunate in the craft of oratory and politicking.

But over the past 75 years or so, the lens through which we view the subject of influence has changed considerably. Increasingly, the process of influence is seen as much as a science as an art, with psychologists, neuroscientists and some noted economists leading the way in its understanding and practice. An important catalyst for this transition occurred in the early months and years after the Second World War. Curiosity frequently follows currency and in the context of a rise in power of the everyday consumer, increased funding was made available for psychological research. Of particular interest to researchers was the role that social and emotional factors play in the influence and change process.

The works of Kurt Lewin, an early pioneer of social and organisational psychology,[8] and Leon Festinger, the psychologist who coined the termed "cognitive dissonance" (the mental toll experienced when we hold contradicting thoughts),[9] rose in prominence sparking an explosion of new research and insights that remain at the heart of how we attempt to influence others today.

Researchers like B.F. Skinner, an American psychologist, reasoned that free will was an illusion. People's actions, Skinner declared, were influenced largely by reinforcement. If the consequences of a previous action were bad, they were unlikely to be repeated. However, should the consequences of a behaviour be good, then the likelihood that the behaviour will be repeated soars.[10] It's a standard that is still adopted, no doubt, by many a frustrated parent.

The Polish-American psychologist Solomon Asch conducted one of psychology's best-known experiments when he asked people to judge the length of a line, but only after witnessing other participants (who were stooges) give a clearly wrong response. In doing so, Asch demonstrated how willing people are to give up their independence in exchange for being accepted into the group.[11] Muzafer Sherif, a Turkish-American social psychologist, was another important contributor. His Robbers Cave experiment demonstrated the role that group dynamics play in shaping behaviour and attitudes.[12] It remains a useful narrative for the polarising and siloed thinking that so frequently blights organisations today.

As the scientific study of influence mushroomed, it increasingly became individualised. Carl Rogers, an early founder of humanistic psychology, developed an approach called "client-centred therapy". In contrast to imposing one's own view, Rogers advocated placing the understanding and acceptance of another's point of view at the front and centre to change.[13] Although his primary interest was in the clinical setting, his ideas caught on in business too. Dale Carnegie's *How to Win Friends and Influence People* had already become a huge success by promoting a similarly client-centred approach.[14] Carnegie, originally a teacher at night school in Manhattan YMCAs, claimed that it was possible to influence people by changing one's behaviour towards them. It is a message that clearly still resonates today. *How to Win Friends and Influence People* is one of the best-selling books of all time and still appears on literary sales charts. Even investor Warren Buffett is a fan, proudly claiming that the only diploma he displays on his office wall is a certificate from one of Carnegie's courses.

But arguably the most important recent contributor to the scientific study of influence is the US psychologist Robert Cialdini. Cialdini says that one of the reasons he became interested in the influence and communication process was his upbringing. Born of Sicilian stock he lived in a predominantly Polish community, in the largely German town of Milwaukee, astride the United States' Great Lakes. Cialdini describes how, as a young child, he needed to adopt a variety of communication strategies to fit in with the wide-ranging cultures and social rules he came across every day. That alone might set the stage for a future inquiring into the human condition. But there was another reason: Cialdini was a self-declared pushover. He frequently described how he was an easy target to any would-be persuader, whether they were seeking to sell tickets to a sanitation workers' annual ball for which he had little enthusiasm, or subscriptions to magazines he was unlikely to ever read. Cialdini's contribution to the modern-day understanding of influence came about because of the simple fact he was a sucker.

Cialdini's 45-year research career into the psychology of persuasion has provided anyone seeking to improve their powers of persuasion with an approach to effective influence that is as potent as it is practical. Beyond economic incentives, Cialdini's claim is that anyone can increase their ability to influence others successfully by aligning their message or request to one of seven universal principles of persuasion.[15]

1. Reciprocity. People feel more obliged to say yes to us if we have done something for them first.
2. Liking. The more we like others and they like us, the more they want to say yes to us.

3. Unity. People will prioritise our requests to the extent to which they see us not just as like them, but as one of them.

4. Authority. People's likelihood to accept our advice and recommendations increases to the extent they perceive us to be an expert.

5. Social proof. People are motivated to follow our proposal when they find others like them are doing the same.

6. Consistency. Our proposals are more persuasive if they align with people's values or a previously made commitment.

7. Scarcity. If our offer is unique or is becoming less available, then people will want it more.

Such is the importance of Cialdini's work, and its practical and meaningful application to the world of work, Chapter 7 is devoted to reviewing each of these principles in more detail.

The new old

In many ways there is nothing new about influence. But in many other ways the influence landscape has changed beyond what the great philosophers and historians could reasonably have foreseen. The advent of the information age and social media has changed the way we influence for ever. Information and data are now freely available at the click of a button or the swipe of a screen. We interact with people in social networks and communities today that we would never have had contact with a generation ago. Gone also are the days where facts and sagacity can be relied upon to trump fiction and stupidity.

The workplace has changed too. Flatter working structures and the advent of the matrix organisation means that position doesn't always mean power. The environment and geography of our interactions have changed too, as they increasingly take place virtually. All these things have forced us to rethink how we communicate with others and influence and persuade them.

The view of influence has changed too. Although unlikely entirely to shake its reputation as a potentially manipulative and scheming practice, many now view it in a more enlightened way. The ability to influence and create change is increasingly being seen as part of the potential answer to the challenges we all face, in our workplaces, our homes, our communities and in the wider society. Because without influence, there is no change.

But what exactly is influence? What are the myths and misperceptions about how to gain influence? And what fundamental human motivations lie at the heart of successful influence and change?

The next chapter addresses these questions.

3

Influence: meanings, myths and motivations

What is influence?

Influence can be defined as the ability to exert or wield an affect or impact on someone or something. The word is derived from the Latin *influens*, which means "flowing in". You can think of influence as a decision, an action or a behaviour taken by a person or persons – as a result of an input or intervention made by someone or something else. That something could be a piece of information or data – like a business proposal, a claim made by a marketer, or a statistic. It might be an incentive for an action (such as a bonus awarded for achieving a sales target) or a penalty for an inaction (like failing to submit your tax return). It could also be an idea or story that triggers an emotional reaction – as when a charity uses images of the impoverished and vulnerable to spur audiences into donating. In short, influence is the effect of changing someone's actions or behaviours at a particular moment in time. This is not the same as persuasion.

Persuasion, from the Latin *persuadere*, means to finalise or take to the point of completion. In contrast to influence, persuasion is better thought of as inner (rather than external) changes that occur over time and that can result in people changing their minds. The distinction between influence and persuasion is important because it is entirely possible to influence people's decisions, actions and behaviours without necessarily persuading them to change their minds. A voter might not care much for any of the candidates vying for election, believing their policies to be as indistinguishable as they are inept. On entering the polling booth, they might vote for the candidate who is most familiar to them or who has a similar sounding name to their own. They have been influenced to act on the basis of a perceived commonality, yet they have not been persuaded to alter their opinion about their chosen candidate.

Although the words "influence" and "persuasion" tend to be used interchangeably (your author is no exception), influence is likely to be the priority for most working professionals – at least initially. And especially if your role requires you to communicate ideas, sell products, engage an audience, solicit help or garner the support of others.

Another reason why influence occupies an ever-present place on lists of desirable workplace skills is because it is seen as an essential tool for managers and leaders. If leadership is the act of getting things done through others, and management is the organising of people and resources to achieve those goals, the ability to influence is at the core of both.

To have influence is to have power. But the reverse is not necessarily true. Lofty titles and superior positions might get you compliance and obedience, but any success gained playing the "boss card" is likely to be temporary, unlikely to win you friends and is generally tiring for everyone concerned. So too is pushing people into a position using manipulative claims and questionable tactics. Such approaches generally lead to resentment, and are likely to diminish any chance of gaining influence in the future.

But nevertheless power is influential. The 15th-century Renaissance political theorist Niccolò Machiavelli noted in *The Prince* that all leaders will struggle to be both loved and feared.[1] And psychologists have long known that people judge others on the basis of two characteristics: warmth and strength. Research finds that 90% of people's impressions of others, whether positive or negative, are based on whether they are seen as warm or strong.[2] My own research, conducted with my colleague Dr Joseph Marks, demonstrates how people will be influenced by one of two types of messenger: hard or soft.[3] The hard messenger is listened to because they are perceived to possess some sort of status over their audience. They might be dominant, possess greater expertise; they might be rich or famous, or physically attractive. In contrast, the soft messenger is listened to because of a connection they share with their audience. They are seen as warm; they might be regarded as vulnerable, trustworthy or charismatic.

Which is best? Machiavelli said the ideal is to be both loved and feared. But when that ideal is not possible, he advocated fear over bonds of love as a more reliable way to inspire discipline. "It is better to be feared than to be loved, if one cannot be both," he noted.

As unappealing as this might sound, many claim Machiavelli was right, at least in certain situations. One way to determine whether a strategy of power and strength will win over a warmer, more connected one concerns which of two kinds of influence a would-be persuader wishes to acquire. One type – *transactional influence* – concerns getting things done. It's the kind of influence where relationships take a back seat to results. It's where an unalloyed, to-the-point communication is prioritised and where strength and conviction are favoured over warmth and the need to be liked.

By contrast, *transformational influence* is concerned with the bigger picture and how actions in the moment can unduly affect larger endeavours. It is the type of influence that attempts to deliver more sustainable outcomes. Influencers who seek to transform, rather than transact, are advised to adopt a softer, more empathetic and encouraging approach over the power play. In a nod to Carnegie's book, they should seek to win friends first and then influence people. A 2014 study of more than 50,000 managers by psychologists Jack Zenger and Joseph Folkman concurs. They found only 27 individuals residing simultaneously in both the bottom quartile of likeability and the top quartile of leadership effectiveness.[4] Put another way, the odds of finding a manager in an organisation who is personally loathed yet held up as a good leader is about one in 2,000.

History shows that the successful influencer tends to be an agile communicator. Someone able to pivot effortlessly between positions of strength and warmth as differing situations and contexts demands. The successful influencer possesses something else too: an understanding of some of the myths and misperceptions of how the influence process works. Three, in particular, are worth a closer look.

Myths and misperceptions 1

Giving information = gaining influence

Consider a typical working day. What time do you get out of bed? 6am? 7am? Maybe later. On that same day, what time do you usually go to bed? 10.30pm? 11pm? Maybe you are more of an owl than a lark. Regardless, there is a pretty good chance you are similar to most working professionals who, on an average working day, are awake for somewhere between 16 and 18 hours.

Now consider this. How many times during those 16–18

hours are you exposed to information that seeks to capture your attention, get you to think about something or act in some way? Consider all the messages and emails you receive. Now consider all the texts, social media posts, newspaper articles, telephone calls and adverts. How about those around you who seek your attention: your partner, your children, your colleagues? And what about work itself? For many of us, the act of clocking on triggers an avalanche of information in the form of data, reports and proposals to wrestle with.

An undeniable feature of daily life is how we are all required to manage a near-constant stream of information directed at us. Some of this information is welcome; most of it is not. History suggests the issue is only set to grow. To provide some perspective, as we entered the 21st century, the average UK citizen was exposed to an estimated 2,000 messages each day (almost double for US citizens). In the early 2010s the internet was rife with claims that those figures had risen to between 10,000 and 30,000 (although it is hard to verify accounts).[5] Some suggest the combination of social media and a smartphone never more than an arm's length away now makes the number almost impossible to count. But that hasn't stopped some researchers trying. A 2021 paper by research firm Datareportal claims the average US citizen spends almost seven hours a day on the internet which, combined with a near-endless array of other offline stimuli such as workplace and home life demands and more ads, totals almost 74GB of data.[6]

The implications of an information-inundated environment for people's decision-making ability and for our ability to influence should be obvious. The capacity of audiences to take on board more information is limited. Yet many seem to forget this, clinging to the notion that if they provide people with information, they will be influenced by that information.

But, rather like pouring water into a bucket that is already full, much of the information directed at us simply flows over the side of our already saturated minds.

This is why the idea that we can simply inform people into change is a misguided one. In fact, there is little to support the idea that the provision of information alone is an effective tool of influence. We inform smokers that they shouldn't smoke. We are told we should exercise more. We are provided with data about why we should eat more healthily, spend less time in front of screens and sleep more. Yet informing people (and ourselves) about the benefits of doing these things (or the perils of not doing them) frequently comes up short. The correlation between the giving of information and gaining of influence is often a weak one.

But I am not suggesting that information is ineffective when it comes to influencing others. In fact information can be very effective, when offered in the right context. It is crucial to understand that when it comes to successful persuasion, it's not necessarily the information itself that matters, but rather how that information is presented. In Chapter 4 I explore three ways to present information in a way that can mean the difference between your message landing persuasively or falling on deaf ears.

However, be in no doubt that if you believe the most productive route to being influential is to inform people into change by providing facts and data, then you should also be prepared, like Sam and Jake, to spend a lot of your time feeling frustrated at people's perceived reluctance to be won over by you.

Myths and misperceptions 2

Changing minds = changing behaviours

In the 1990s, barely one in ten Americans believed it was important to follow the advice of health experts and eat five portions of fruit and vegetables a day. In an attempt to address the issue, the United States Department of Agriculture spent millions of dollars over the next decade on campaigns designed to change minds. At first glance it appeared the money was well spent. A large follow-up survey conducted in 2002 showed how beliefs had shifted. Compared with the previous decade's one in ten, research showed that now 35% of US citizens believed it was important to eat the recommended five daily portions.[7] Yet sales figures from retailers showed that consumption of fruit and vegetables had not changed at all.

This is a common finding in influence research. There are often inconsistencies between people's attitudes and beliefs and their behaviours. I live a short distance from London in a suburban area that Ofsted (a government body responsible for inspecting education services) reports has good schools. As a consequence, many families move to the area in the hope of winning a prized place at a good school for their children. Walking to the railway station in the mornings, it is interesting to observe the behaviour of parents dropping their kids off at these schools. Some double park on roads, holding up traffic. Others mount the pavement, ensuring their precious offspring are delivered as close to the entrance gates as possible, causing pedestrians – including other parents with young children – to navigate circuitous routes through a maze of vehicles while inhaling lungsful of air spewed from large gas-guzzling SUVs. Many of these vehicles have "Save the planet" stickers and other pledges of support for environmental protection affixed to bumpers and windscreens.

But perhaps the inconsistency is understandable. The drivers are keen to declare their alignment with a popular and socially approved of belief – that it is good to protect the environment. But they also want to be good, caring parents and so when they face the much more immediate (and conflicting) goal of delivering Johnny and Sally safely to the school gates, the children take priority.

Examples abound where a need to accomplish a specific goal requires us to act in a way that is inconsistent with a broader attitude or belief we possess, or at least want others to think we have. Many people hold strong political views such as societal fairness yet deviate from those beliefs by supporting a political policy that fuels inequality. Despite believing it important to live within one's means, many succumb to the instant gratification of a weekend trip to the shops. And, despite knowing the consequences of putting off until tomorrow something we really should be doing today, we all procrastinate.

To be seen by others as consistent is a desirable human trait that boosts our sense of self-esteem. Indeed, most of us prefer to act in ways that are in line with our attitudes and beliefs. So it's an easy leap to believe the same must be true of others and think that, to change people's decisions and actions, we must first change their minds. But changing people's minds is hard. For an illustration of how hard, ask yourself the question that polarisation experts Alison Goldsworthy, Laura Osbourne and Alex Chesterfield pose to guests in their popular podcast *Changed My Mind*. "When was the last time you changed your mind about something important?" Don't be surprised if, like many of their guests, you struggle to answer.

Although changing people's minds is hard, when it comes to influencing their decisions and behaviours, it is often unnecessary. Yes, you read that correctly. It is not always necessary to change people's minds for us to influence their actions and behaviours, as a 2022 study carried out by two of my Influence at Work colleagues illustrates.

With their overly long tongues, pointy noses and scaly bodies, pangolins – insect-eating mammals indigenous to sub-Saharan Africa – are not the prettiest of creatures. But their unappealing features do not make them any less attractive to the poachers and traffickers who boil off their scales to use in Chinese medicine remedies before peddling the leftover carcasses to unprincipled restaurants as an off-the-menu, highly illegal delicacy. The practice is large and widespread. The World Wide Fund for Nature (WWF), a conservation charity, estimates that almost a quarter of a million pangolins are butchered annually.[8]

Issues like poaching and wildlife trafficking are notoriously difficult to tackle. Many practices trace their origins back to long-held customs and deeply embedded cultural beliefs. For some impoverished communities the practice, although illegal and repulsive, might be one of only a few reliable sources of revenue available. Corruption plays a part; so too does the sheer scale of the challenge. There are thousands of poachers and traffickers operating on an industrial scale. Interpol, the international criminal police organisation, estimates the market to be worth more than $20bn a year.[9]

Complex, multifaceted and often culturally ingrained problems call for a wide range of policies and approaches to confront them. Coalitions between governments to reduce corruption can help. So can partnerships between private organisations and not-for-profits to develop, invest in and promote alternative and more sustainable living arrangements. It is also important to reduce demand for illegally traded wildlife by actually influencing the behaviours of those who consume them, rather than just attempting to change their minds.

This is precisely what Eloise Copland and Olivia Pattison, two behavioural scientists, have been successfully doing in communities across Vietnam. In partnership with local non-government organisations, they trialled a variety of influence techniques designed to persuade restaurant-goers to stop ordering pangolin and other illegal bushmeats from under-the-counter menus. These persuasive appeals, which included a message stating that most people don't eat wildmeat and another stating that those who do are highly disapproved of, reduced the consumption of wildmeat by almost 50%.[10]

Following the trials Copland and Pattison conducted post-study surveys and implicit association tests (assessments designed to detect subconscious associations) to see whether the reduction in consumption they recorded resulted in any change in attitudes or beliefs towards eating trafficked meat. It didn't. Despite successfully changing the behaviours of some restaurant-goers, their beliefs and attitudes remained unerringly fixed.

As much as people might like to think of themselves as flexible, adaptable beings who constantly update their beliefs and attitudes, the reality is often different. Change is hard. For those of us challenged with influencing people at work it is important to remember this. As much as we might like to convince people that their perspective is wrong and ours is right, it is a mindset and approach that rarely produces desired results.

It is also worth reminding ourselves that many of the influence challenges we face at work require us to win only the outcome, not necessarily the argument. Winning the outcome doesn't necessarily require us to change minds, but only decisions and behaviours, which tend to be more malleable and flexible. Of course, if you manage to change someone's behaviour and their minds also start to catch up, then consider that the icing on your cake.

Just don't count on it.

Myths and misperceptions 3

Ask people what will persuade them

Compared with the commentary of contemporary business sages like Warren Buffett, Bill Gates and Charles Handy, the musings of Greek philosophers rarely feature in the communication, management and sales training programmes taking place in boardrooms and corporate retreats around the world. There is one rumination, however, that the consultants and coaches responsible for equipping workers with these skills regularly cite.

Epictetus, a Stoic in the third century BC, judged that the role of any human life was to hone and prioritise the virtue of character. He believed material factors such as fame, fortune and reputation should be viewed as indifferent to the primary goal of a good life lived. It was Epictetus who observed "that to possess two ears and only one mouth is a God-given sign one should listen more than one speaks".[11]

One can only speculate how Epictetus would react to learning how his quote has become a staple used to inspire professionals to achieve the very fame and fortune he viewed as meaningless. His observation, nonetheless, is well made. Many agree that the world would be a better place if people followed Epictetus's advice and listened more. I do too, but with one important caveat.

A common finding from decades of persuasion research

is how poor people are at identifying the factors most likely to influence their future actions and behaviours. So although I certainly agree how important it is to ask people what will likely influence them and to listen carefully to their answers, I also advise you do not routinely accept their responses at face value.

A good example comes from a series of studies conducted by Wesley Schultz, Jessica Nolan, Robert Cialdini, Noah Goldstein and Vladas Griskevicius.[12] Homeowners in Southern California were asked to rank four messages designed to persuade them to reduce their energy consumption, in order of persuasiveness. One message communicated how conserving energy would contribute to the broader need to reduce emissions in society. A second stated that, by conserving energy today, they would be protecting future generations; essentially the message was: "Do it for your children and grandkids." A third message highlighted how much money a typical household would save by reducing their energy consumption. A fourth took a different approach and simply informed households that many of their neighbours were already finding ways to conserve energy.

Households resoundingly rated the message stating how their efforts would contribute to the broader societal goal as the most motivating and most likely to influence their actions. Next most persuasive was the future generations message. Third was the money-saving message. The message pointing out that their neighbours were finding ways to conserve energy was rated the least motivating or persuasive.

The researchers, however, were not so convinced, and so they devised a clever experiment. Over the course of several weeks, they arranged for households to be exposed to one of the four messages in the form of signs placed near their front doors. Some residents saw a message stating that conserving energy saves the environment. Another group observed a message describing the benefit to future generations. Others were told how much money they could save by conserving energy. A fourth group saw a message informing them that many of their neighbours were actively conserving energy. Over the next month, meter readings were captured and recycling was weighed to measure the influence of each message and its impact on the desired action.

Remember most people reported that the message about protecting the environment was the one most likely to persuade them to conserve energy. Yet those exposed to this message didn't change at all. The "Do it for the kids" and the "Do it to save money" messages fared no better. When it came to influencing a change, the only message that had any meaningful impact was the neighbours' message that the householders had roundly rejected as having no sway whatsoever.

Not only are people poor at recognising what will influence their future decisions and actions; they are just as likely to be blind to what persuaded them when they are asked to reflect after the event. A few years ago, one of my colleagues was invited as a guest on a current affairs TV show to talk about when and why people are likely to help others in everyday, non-emergency situations. The TV crew had previously been out on the streets filming footage for the studio discussion. One film reel was recorded at a busy junction where observers counted the number of passing commuters who gave money to a street musician performing near the entrance of a railway station. Few did. That was until someone, a stooge, dropped some money into the performer's hat in full view of approaching travellers. Immediately, the observers counted an eight-fold increase in the number of commuters who, having seen someone else give money, donated too.

But perhaps the most entertaining feature of the pre-recorded film were the interviews afterwards. Not one commuter attributed their actions to seeing someone else give money first. Instead, they provided a series of alternative (and entirely incorrect) reasons for their actions. "I'm a generous person." "I felt sorry for the guy." "He was playing a song I like."

The fact that most people aren't that good at recognising the factors influencing their decisions and actions, both before and after an event, poses a dilemma to those of us interested in persuading them. The time, effort and potentially considerable cost of engaging colleagues, clients or customers in conversations about what will persuade them might result in some unreliable responses. To be clear, the advice here is *not* to stop asking. The risk of damaging a meaningful connection and potential fruitful relationship is a good enough reason to listen carefully to their replies. Rather, the advice is to be aware of the potential that their responses to your questions might be rose-tinted. Viewing them through a (thinnish) veneer of scepticism could be useful. So can keeping in mind Epictetus's observation that we have twice as many tools for receiving information as we do for transmitting it. Asking a few clarifying questions to probe and delve a little deeper is generally a good practice.

Motivations: why people decide, act and change

If trying to inform people into change is unreliable, attempting to change people's minds in the hope that they will change their behaviour is tiring and largely ineffective, and asking people what will persuade them is undependable, what can those of us seeking to influence others do that might be more effective? One approach is to ensure that our requests, proposals and offers appeal to one of just a small number of fundamental human motivations central to us all. They are *accuracy*, *connection* and *ego*.

The late Lord Grade of Elstree was reputedly fond of telling a story about a young man who came to his office one day to interview for a job. It was 7.30am and the peer, puffing on his second Havana of the morning, stared intently at the jobseeker for a few moments before picking up a large jug of water and placing it on the middle of his desk. "Young man," he said, "I have been reliably informed that you are quite the persuader. So, sell me this jug of water."

Undaunted, the young man rose from his chair and walked towards the corner of the room where he picked up a wastepaper basket full to the brim with discarded documents. Placing it on the desk next to the jug of water, he stared intently at his elder for a few seconds before calmly striking a match and dropping it into the basket. As the flames mushroomed to an unnerving height, the young man turned to his potential employer and asked: "How much will you give me for this jug of water?"[13]

The story offers a useful lesson to anyone who wants to be more influential. To make the sale, the young man did not seek to persuade Lord Grade by pointing out specific facts or features about the jug. Nor did he introduce any financial incentive. Instead, he simply changed the context in which the jug of water was offered. No longer was it a potentially refreshing, thirst-quenching drink. Now it was a much-needed tool to deal with a spiralling blaze. The young man, who got the job, had cleverly understood how it is possible to influence the decisions and actions of others by changing the psychological context of his proposal so that it aligned with a fundamental human motivation.

The specific motivation that was triggered by the young

man was *accuracy*. Accuracy describes the deep-seated and fundamental human motivation to do what seems to be the right thing within the context and constraints that we are operating in at the time. In the context of the growing inferno on his desk, Lord Grade's immediate motivation was to do the accurate thing by extinguishing the fire. As a consequence it was instantly prioritised in his mind. Accuracy is the first of three fundamental motivations. The other two, *connection* (the motivation to act in ways that connect us to others) and *ego* (the desire to behave in ways that allow us to feel good about ourselves and our actions), are worth committing to memory because they reside, either singly or in combination, at the heart of all successful influence strategies. And they handily also come packaged in an easily recalled mnemonic: ACE.

Before looking at each of these three motivations in turn, let's consider why they are so central to the process of influence and persuasion. Imagine you are standing in the middle of a dark, windowless room. It's pitch black. Fortunately, you are aware of a light switch on the wall that you can reach out and touch. You flick the switch and the room immediately illuminates. What caused the lights to come on? The flicking of the switch, right? Well, not quite. The switch doesn't provide the electrical power. What powers the lights is the electricity in the system. The switch simply completes the circuit between the electricity and the light bulb. Activating the switch if there was no power available would achieve nothing.

The accuracy, connection and ego motivations work in a similar way. Rather like the power in an electrical system, each of these motivations is already installed in people, ready to be called upon when the right switch is triggered. However, unlike the power in an electrical system, these human motivations cannot be turned off. They are always available. Successful influencers know this and recognise the fundamental role they play in influencing decisions and how to trigger them.

The accuracy motivation: people's desire to do the right thing

In the complex, information-overloaded and uncertain world where we live, people are motivated to be accurate with their perceptions, their decisions and their actions. Failure to do so can place them in a position where they might miss out on potential benefits and rewards. Worse, they could expose themselves to serious threats, risks and losses. Put another way, people want to make what seem to be the "right" choices.

But the decisions we make are not always based on a deliberative calculation of the costs and benefits of every option presented to us. Few of us have the time or energy for that. Nor are our decisions made on the basis of balanced information, primarily because information is rarely balanced. Facts are frequently manipulated and sometimes manufactured entirely. Data and figures are often presented in ways that allow them to shine. In describing the persuasive power of numbers to boost an otherwise weak argument, Mark Twain observed that there are three kinds of lies: "there are lies, there are damned lies, and then there are statistics".

The sheer volume of information, coupled with the frequent and legitimate concerns about its integrity, means making accurate decisions is hard. Consequently, when attempting to make the right decision people tend to fall back on a few tried and trusted clues and cues to guide their actions. Rather than evaluating the credibility of all the available information and weighing it up in a computational fashion, people tend to do what Herbert Simon, a Nobel laureate in Economic Sciences, described as *satisfice*.[14] They seek the first available satisfactory and sufficient solution to a problem or issue. A diner in a restaurant might choose the sommelier's choice because "wine experts know their stuff". A finance manager, on being presented with a proposal that seems too good to be true, might consider that it probably is and reject it. And rather than switching investments to a higher paying scheme, a pensioner might keep their savings in a long-held but lower-paying account because "better the devil you know than the devil you don't".

The effective influencer recognises and includes in their proposals, appeals and communications cues and signals that trigger the accuracy motivation. What these cues and signals are will be different dependent on the context. Part 2 describes many of them with advice on how to use them effectively and ethically.

The connection motivation: people's desire to do the right thing for others

The connection motivation influences people to act and make decisions, not necessarily based on an evaluation of the facts and finances but on whether the actions and decisions they take will help them create, or maintain, a positive bond with others. And, ideally, gain their approval too. Connection is a powerful motivational force because humans are the most social of creatures compelled to create and maintain positive social bonds with others.

Success rarely occurs as a result of isolation. More likely, it is a result of the quality and number of social connections and relationships with others. People frequently prioritise their connections with others when deciding what to do. They do this even when the idea is not an especially good one.

There's a story about a family in Texas sitting in the shade outside their house one hot summer afternoon.[15] The father-in-law, who was visiting the family, suggests they drive to the town of Abilene, almost 50 miles away, for dinner. "Good idea," the mother says. Her husband, despite his misgivings about a two-hour round trip in an overcrowded car, keeps his thoughts to himself and acquiesces. "I'm happy to go if your mum wants to." The mother-in-law replies: "Sure, sounds like fun. Let's go."

On arriving at Abilene, the family finds the service and food at the diner is as miserable as their journey. They return home four hours later, exhausted and on edge. In an attempt to inject some positivity into an otherwise rotten excursion, one of the family remarks how much he enjoyed the trip. The mother-in-law says that, given the time again, she would have stayed at home. Everyone else agrees.

"Then why did we go?"

"I only suggested it because I thought you might be bored."

"I only went because you seemed keen."

Confounded, they go to bed, wondering why they decided to take a trip no one wanted, instead of spending an agreeable laze in the afternoon sun they were already enjoying.

Termed the Abilene paradox, this situation demonstrates how a desire to feel connected to and gain the approval of others can frequently crowd out more considered, accurate thinking. And its occurrence is not restricted solely to families. To avoid being contrary, many people at work may prioritise connectedness over accuracy, often to the detriment of a project they are working on being delivered more efficiently.

The Abilene paradox has parallels to another phenomenon – groupthink – but is not the same. The Abilene paradox occurs when a group of people collectively agree on an action or pursuit that individually no one would choose, mistakenly believing that it is what everyone else wants. Groupthink occurs when a group of people seek consensus and in doing so make decisions based on incomplete information, limited critical thinking or outside advice.[16]

Of course, I am not suggesting that decisions and actions influenced as a result of the connection motivation are suboptimal or unworthy. Frequently the opposite is true. The trust that people have in companies is frequently predicated on how connected they feel to them. Many who work in healthcare – rarely a handsomely remunerated vocation – do so because of the emotional connection the job provides. Some people might even ignore their own needs to form connections with wider groups outside their immediate family and friends. During the coronavirus pandemic, many vaccination appeals directed attention not to the individual benefits of getting vaccinated, but on the importance of protecting others. Evidence suggests that these appeals were often successful with many people, despite personally held misgivings, rolling up their sleeves because it seemed like the right thing to do for the wider good.

The effective influencer recognises that engaging others via the connection motivation requires them to build a bridge between the merits of the case they wish to make and the impact that the case will have on the person or people concerned. They also appear acutely aware of how these connections come about, not from emotionless data and bloodless statistics but rather from meaningful, emotionally charged stories.

If you need any further convincing of the power of meaningful stories in making a connection, perhaps reflect on your own experiences. Notice how many times people have happily argued and rebutted the data and statistics you have provided to support a case. But notice, too, how these same people will argue with you less when you tell your story. Effective influencers are effective connectors. They paint pictures and present compelling images. They describe accounts not of efficiencies counted and balance sheets boosted but of lives changed and crucial connections to others made.

The ego motivation: people's desire to do the right thing for themselves

As well as being motivated to do what seems to be the right thing (accuracy) and to do the right thing for others (connection), people are also motivated to act in ways that allow them to feel good about themselves. This is the ego motivation.

Lots of evidence documents the strong motivation people have to think favourably about themselves. When asked, more than three-quarters of people claim to be a better than average driver.[17] Impossible, of course. Nearly half of these people even claim a place in the top 20% of drivers. Also impossible. These findings hold true across different countries and cultures, emphasising how fundamental the desire to be seen in a positive light is.

This is not to say that people are narcissists. Some people might be, but most satisfy the desire to hold a worthy view of themselves not by focusing on the way they look, the things they buy or the cars they (expertly) drive, but by living up to their commitments and acting consistently with their self-ascribed traits and sense of identity.

Understanding this can be helpful to anyone interested in persuading others. A pre-covid experiment carried out with doctors found that they were much more likely to sanitise their hands between patient examinations if they were reminded that they had taken the Hippocratic oath than when they were given messages about reducing cross-contamination and the risk of personal infection.[18] Rather than informing them into compliance, the medics were nudged by aligning the desired action (handwashing) with an existing commitment (the oath they take to do no harm). Acting consistently with that previous commitment could allow them to feel good about themselves and to see themselves in a positive light.

At the core of any successful influence attempt is one or more of these three fundamental motivations. Successful persuaders know this and when designing an influence strategy are careful to ask themselves several questions. Does the proposal I am making seem like the accurate thing to do for my audience? Will what I am proposing appear to be the connected thing for my audience to do? Does my offer give the person I am persuading an ego boost and allow them to feel better about themselves?

Arguably the most effective appeals will trigger all three of the fundamental motivations. Ride-sharing apps like Uber and Lyft do exactly this. Instead of people standing outside in the rain waving at passing cars, looking for the taxi they ordered, apps helpfully provide a cue of "accuracy" by way of the little car icon on the map accompanied by the licence plate number. Passengers are also informed in advance of the estimated cost – another cue of accuracy that eliminates the uncertainty often felt in a metered taxi. The name and photograph of the driver, with information about how other users have rated him or her, provides a helpful "connection". Apps also provide reassurance by signalling the number of previous trips the driver has completed safely. Even the "ego" motivation is suitably catered for. By timing their departure from the pub precisely when their taxi pulls up outside, anyone can feel – albeit for a moment – like a celebrity.

For anyone interested in influencing others, which is all of us, the implications should be clear. Although evidence and economics remain crucial elements of any influence strategy, their success in convincing and persuading others depends on the emotional connection that a communicator makes. The fundamental motivations of accuracy, connection and ego are core to doing just that.

The Influence Equation

Received wisdom suggests that the most effective way to influence others is to make an offer or proposition comprising the best evidence and the most appealing economic incentives. Reality proves this is not always the case. Evidence and information, although crucial, isn't always enough to convince others. Economic factors, like financial incentives, are an important part too but like information are often only part of the story. Human emotions matter also. The feelings that people experience when one of the fundamental motivations of accuracy, connection and ego is triggered play a central role in what they choose to say yes to, and what they reject. This is true whether the goal is persuading a single individual, a group of people or an entire organisation or country.

Consequently, successful approaches to influence and persuasion need to take account of all three of these important factors. This book provides it in the form of an Influence Equation.

In the 17th and 18th centuries, the pioneers Sir Isaac Newton and Johann Wolfgang von Goethe theorised that any colour could be created by combining varying quantities of one of three primary colours – red, yellow and blue. The Influence Equation works in a similar way. Just as it is possible to create an array of different colours by combining different proportions of three primary colours, you can create successful influence strategies by combining the optimal quantities of Evidence + Economics + Emotion appropriate to the context in which you are working (see Figure 1).

Figure 1: **The Influence Equation**

$$\text{influence} = \frac{\text{evidence} + \text{economics} + \text{emotion}}{\text{context}}$$

Precisely what the best combination will be will depend on the specific context you find yourself in. Part 2 describes the most persuasive ways to present evidence (Chapter 4), to structure economic incentives (Chapter 5) and to trigger emotional reactions (Chapter 6). The result is an approach that will enable you to craft effective influence strategies for any influence challenge you encounter at work – and at home too.

PART 2

The Influence Equation

Overview

Imagine one day you receive a call from a friend giddy with excitement about some news she has just received. She explains that, a few weeks ago, she applied for a job at a well-known organisation that owns several high-profile brands. It's her dream job. She's excited because she has just received an email from the recruiter informing her that she is one of four candidates shortlisted for a final interview.

But before you get the chance to congratulate your friend, her tone suddenly changes. Sounding serious, she explains how she desperately needs your advice.

"All the interviews are going to be held on the same day next week. And I've been given the choice of when I will be interviewed. I don't know what to do. Should I go first? First impressions count, don't they? But maybe second would be better? Or should I go third? Perhaps I go last and hope I'm the candidate they remember the most. I need to call the recruiter back and I simply don't know. Please help me."

What do you advise your friend to do?

*

The job interview is a good example of influence at work. Both recruiter and wannabe recruits are motivated to have a persuasive effect on each other. Consequently, all parts of the Influence Equation are at play. The recruiter is seeking *evidence* that candidates have the necessary capabilities to do the job.

They will ask potential employees to share their credentials and seek examples of how and where they have demonstrated skills deemed important to the job. Candidates will want to reassure themselves that the role they are applying for is a good career fit. They will be looking for evidence their potential new employer can offer a fulfilling role with the appropriate opportunities for personal and professional growth.

The *economics* are important too. Recruiters want to attract the best candidates within the constraints of what's affordable. Jobseekers, invariably, are motivated to seek the highest remuneration, though not necessarily at any cost. Work–life balance, personal development and a sense of purpose are important too and will likely be priced into their thinking.

So too will *emotions*. Sometimes hirers and the hired just get a good sense about each other. Similarities, positive first impressions and a feeling of "being on the same wavelength" often emerge early in interviews and can exert a heavy influence on decisions. In situations like this, it is hard to resist the persuasive pull of something *feeling* like the right thing to do.

In addition to the Influence Equation's numerators of *evidence, economics* and *emotion,* it is important to consider its denominator: *context*. Context is always a crucial consideration for the would-be persuader. Again, the job interview provides a helpful example. One obvious context concerns the ebbs and flows of the employment market. If the pool of suitable talent is small, recruiters will need to adjust accordingly. They might have to temper the amount of evidence needed before being convinced of a candidate's suitability. They might need to pay more. And any desire they harbour to employ the scarcer, emotionally "right" candidate might need to be revised in favour of the available "right-now" candidate.

But when there is an abundance of suitable talent, the

context changes. Fortune now favours the employer who is in the enviable position of a surfeit of willing and skilled applicants. The pendulum of influence swings away from the jobseeker and now a heavier burden rests on their shoulders: to persuade the recruiter that, of myriad choices available, they are the best candidate.

Of course, the job interview is just one example of thousands of influence challenges we might face in our professional and personal lives. And although each challenge will vary in some way and depend on the context, there are commonalties. For example, many of the challenges a recruiter faces in trying to persuade jobseekers to apply to join their business exist in other scenarios. Like a business development executive attempting to win a new client, or a doctor trying to persuade a patient to take their medication, or a teacher convincing their class to hand in homework assignments on time. This means that even though every influence challenge will appear unique, the framework we use to address that challenge can be the same.

The Influence Equation is that framework. It asserts that successful influence is achieved by presenting your case founded on the right combination of evidence, economics and emotions while considering the context in which you are working. Part 2 of this book describes effective ways to deploy this trio of factors, devoting a chapter to each. It also offers a perspective on the advice you offered to that excited, job-seeking friend of yours.

4

Influencing with evidence

In the mid-20th century, with consumer demand rising, Ford – the US-based car behemoth – wanted to speed up the production of gearboxes for its most popular models. So it struck a deal with Mazda – a Japanese counterpart – to bolster its manufacturing capability. Shortly after the ink had dried on contracts and cars were rolling off Detroit production lines and into showrooms, something strange happened. Customers began requesting cars with the Japanese-made transmissions rather than US ones. Despite parts all being made to the exact same specifications, American consumers seemed so convinced of the superiority of the Japanese parts that they were willing to wait months longer for vehicles containing them.

The explanation can be traced back to a quiet revolution that had started in Tokyo at the end of the Second World War, led by a little-known statistics professor from New York named William Edwards Deming.

Deming had pioneered a data-based approach to manufacturing with Japanese industries called statistical process control (SPC). The process used real-time evidence to monitor and control the quality of manufacturing.[1] Some believe that SPC was the forerunner of what many today call "evidence-based management". It appears that the American family's preference for US-branded cars with Japanese parts was, in part, influenced by a perception that anything created on the basis of good evidence was more worthy.[2] As Deming himself is said to have remarked before being awarded the National Medal of Technology and Innovation by President Ronald Reagan:

"In God we trust. Everyone else must bring data." (aka evidence)

It is a philosophy that has been widely embraced in the workplace. We live in a world of evidence-based decision-making. A near-universal narrative now exists in organisations, big and small: "If you want to get your ideas heard and your proposals accepted, present the evidence."

No surprise, then, that evidence is a crucial component of the influence process, informing how arguments are made and decisions are reached. Evidence is vital in helping decision-makers to assess the strength and reliability of arguments and perspectives. Evidence allows audiences to differentiate between reliable facts and flaky fiction.

Yet we can all recall times when our audience has remained unconvinced by our arguments, choosing to favour an alternative proposal or do nothing at all. And this happens despite us possessing a good case founded on solid evidence.

In this chapter I will demonstrate how you can improve your influence at work by ensuring that the evidence you offer in support of your ideas and appeals is presented in a compelling and persuasive way. I am going to assume you have a good, evidence-based case to make. (If you don't, then fix that first.) What I will show you are three ways (founded on evidence) that can increase the attractiveness of the case you are making. Importantly, this won't require you to change the evidence itself but, rather, how you present it.

But before we explore these three approaches, let's first define what we mean by evidence.

What is evidence?

Evidence refers to any information, data or source that supports or refutes a claim, theory or idea.[3] Perhaps controversially, I include in this definition information that may not be verifiable or factually true. Not because I advocate the use of falsehoods to persuade others, but because living in an information-overwhelmed society makes it difficult to determine what should be listened to and what can reliably be dismissed.

Evidence can broadly be categorised in three ways:[4]

- empirical
- expert
- anecdotal.

Empirical evidence should be regarded as the most reliable because it is founded on the collection and analysis of first-hand information such as tests, experiments, observations, statistics and surveys. The strength of empirical evidence as a tool of influence lies in its objectivity and concreteness. Despite this, audiences may call into question the reliability of empirical evidence by raising concerns about the experimental methods employed, the representativeness of those studied or the significance of the results. Some audiences may even question the impartiality of the researchers themselves.

Expert evidence refers to the testimony and opinions of those perceived to have advanced training, knowledge and wisdom about a particular subject matter. Often used in legal proceedings and public body reviews, evidence from experts can be influential because it is commonly viewed as coming from a source of authority and credibility. Commonly, but not always. Some audiences might be sceptical about particular experts, especially if they believe them to have a personal bias or are beholden to certain others. Increasingly (and disappointingly) some experts might be viewed as holding personal views and perspectives incompatible with their audience – despite that mismatch having no relevance to the matter being discussed.

Anecdotes too can be viewed as evidence.[5] Founded on tales and narratives, anecdotes are often the result of a memorable experience or the passing down of stories. Sometimes anecdotes are context-dependent, so might not be widely applicable. Frequently, they are elaborated and embellished over time as they pass from person to person. In the process they become variations and interpretations that possess little in common with the original. Raymond Wolfinger, a US political scientist, noted that the plural of anecdote is not data. But that doesn't make anecdotes any less compelling or persuasive. If anything, as we will explore in Chapter 6, they become more so.

Recall that having a good case to make is not the same as making a case well. This prompts a question: what can any would-be influencer do to ensure that any evidence in support of their case is presented in the most effective way?

Research tells us that three things matter a great deal.

1. How evidence is presented, aka the framing.
2. Who presents the evidence, aka the messenger.
3. The right amount of evidence, aka the rule of three.

Let's look at each in turn.

The framing

If you want to appear tall, it helps to have short friends

As a behavioural scientist best known for my work in the psychology of influence and persuasion, I am fortunate to interact with a wide range of people across a vast array of projects. From elected officials and policymakers to business executives and public sector workers, almost everyone, it seems, has a keen interest in learning how to influence and change the behaviours of others. Including those working in professional sport.

I am a keen football fan and am lucky to occasionally work with some of the sport's best-known coaches and players. The interactions are always memorable but there is one in particular that looms large in my memory. A few years ago, a group of managers and former players attended a development day hosted by one of the major football associations. I was invited to lead a session on the role influence and persuasion plays in managing players and coaching staff. It was a stimulating conversation. I remember being both impressed by the quality of the discussion and pleasantly surprised at how relevant the subject matter seemed to those attending. So relevant, it seemed, that during the lunch break I was approached by a high-profile former premier league player keen to share a story.

He told me about a time when he arrived at his team's stadium early one morning to find workmen working in the corridor outside the players' dressing rooms. One was putting down groundsheets to protect the floor. Two others were standing behind him – one holding a crowbar and a saw, the other grappling with a wooden architrave. A fourth, holding a tin of white paint and a brush, made up the troupe. After exchanging pleasantries (and posing for a photo and autograph), the player casually asked what the men were doing.

"We're working on the doors and frames of the changing rooms," one replied.

"They look OK to me," said the footballer. "Why replace them?"

"Oh we're not replacing them," said another workmen. "We're *adjusting* them."

The workmen went on to explain that they had been instructed to lower the door frame of the home team's dressing room by a couple of inches, and raise the frame of the visiting team's dressing room by the same amount.

As I listened to the story, I couldn't help but laugh at the brilliant audacity of the strategy. Imagine the visiting team, glancing at the home team as they entered their dressing room, noticing how many were having to duck their heads. Now imagine what went through their minds when they realised they did not need to do the same as they entered theirs.

"Oh my God," some of them, even fleetingly, might have thought. "These guys must be giants!"

Ethics and fair play aside, the story has become one of my favourite examples of a phenomenon that anyone wishing to persuade others needs to understand. We can call it *framing*. Or, perhaps in the case of my footballer friend, door-framing.

What comes first, often matters most

There's a common mistake many of us make when attempting to persuade others. It's to fall into the trap of thinking all that's needed to convince others is some good evidence, together with a reason. However, there is a problem with this approach. It neglects an obvious, yet frequently overlooked, feature of human decision-making: how hard we find it to decide in the absence of a comparison.

We all use comparisons to determine the relative worth of

something. An average-looking house can appear really nice if the one next door is in a state of disrepair. Yet that same house might appear pretty shabby if next door is palatial. Nothing changes about the house itself; what has changed is what it is compared with. Presumably that's why a scheming property agent might drive prospective clients through the rougher parts of town on the way to a viewing. Compared with what the clients see first, an entirely average destination might seem like a paradise.

Comparisons are omnipresent. Look at the two wine lists in Figure 2. All the information (evidence) on each list is the same. So too are the prices (economics). The only difference is how the lists are presented. One has the cheapest wine at the top, with each subsequent option increasing in price. The other starts with the most expensive, with subsequent options descending in price. Given that the evidence and the economics are the same, it is logical to assume that both lists

Figure 2: **Comparing wine lists**

WINE LIST	
HOUSE WINE	£7.50
WINE A	**£8.00**
WINE B	**£8.50**
WINE C	£9.00
WINE D	£9.50
WINE E	£10.00
WINE F	£10.50
WINE G	£11.00
WINE H	£11.50

WINE LIST	
WINE H	£11.50
WINE G	£11.00
WINE F	£10.50
WINE E	**£10.00**
WINE D	**£9.50**
WINE C	**£9.00**
WINE B	£8.50
WINE A	£8.00
HOUSE WINE	£7.50

will result in the same choice decisions. But that's not what happens. Assuming people read lists from top to bottom, those seeing the higher priced wine first often go on to choose a more expensive wine. But those exposed to the cheapest wine first, frequently choose a lower-priced option.[6]

The concept of framing – first directing attention to one thing to make a subsequent choice or option appear more different – is a mainstay of effective persuasion.[7]

My colleague Oded Netzer, a professor of business and author of the excellent *Decisions Over Decimals*, at the Columbia Business School, offers this example of framing to his MBA students. A union representing office cleaners is demanding pay rises for its members whose salaries have fallen beyond those of managers. This sounds reasonable and the evidence supports the union's case (see Figure 3a).

Figure 3a: **Office cleaners' salaries are falling behind**

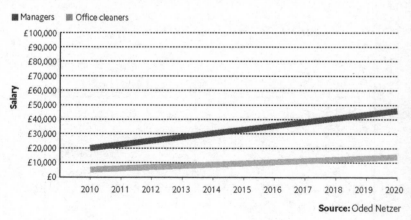

Source: Oded Netzer

Netzer then presents the salary comparison on a logarithmic scale. Despite the data being the same, presenting it in this way suggests the disparity the union is highlighting is already narrowing (see Figure 3b).

Figure 3b: **But the gap with managers' pay is narrowing**

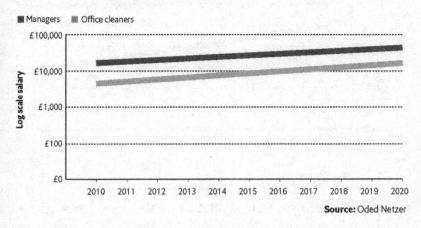

Source: Oded Netzer

When Netzer presents the evidence as a salary index scale (see Figure 3c) and then as a year-on-year scale (Figure 3d), it's the managers, not the cleaners, who appear to have a legitimate claim for a pay rise.

Figure 3c: **The salary index shows the opposite**

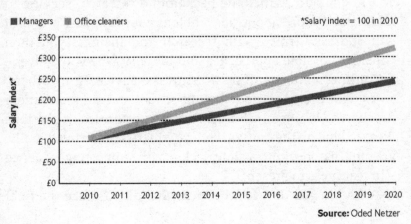

Source: Oded Netzer

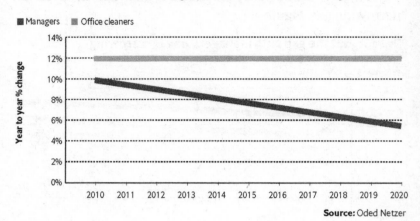

Figure 3d: **Year on year, managers' salaries are decreasing**

Source: Oded Netzer

It is an example that invariably causes executives to nod knowingly, perhaps reflecting that they themselves might have previously succumbed. Netzer's point is a crucial one. What we compare our evidence with determines the narrative, not the evidence itself. It is especially important to remember this when presenting ideas and proposals.

Consider the typical steps taken to construct a proposal. You might start with some background research, seeking to understand more about the problem your eventual proposal will address. Armed with research and insights you then consider possible approaches and ideas. Maybe you convene an online whiteboard session to ask advice from others. You might even choose to go old-school and stand around a flipchart to brainstorm ideas. Next you prioritise the various ideas to land on the one you believe will best fit the bill. Finally, you put that idea into a slide deck – with supporting evidence – in readiness to present.

What do you do with the ideas that didn't make the final

cut? Like many people, you probably consign them to the bin. Understandable? Yes. A mistake? Also, yes. Although those ideas may have lost their value as the centrepiece of your proposal, they are not entirely worthless. In fact, they now represent a new kind of value. They become a legitimate opportunity for comparison, allowing you to frame your selected idea in a way that allows it to shine. Here's how.

Imagine you are presenting your chosen proposal to a prospective client or a finance director at budget time. You might say something like this.

> "As you would expect, in preparing for today's meeting we did our research, during which three ideas emerged. We took a detailed look at each of them. We concluded that one of the ideas might have some unintended consequences, making it too much of a risk. And having done the numbers, we calculated that the second idea was likely to come in over budget. For these reasons, we strongly recommend that we focus on this third idea."

Notice how the ideas you might previously have dismissed now act as a legitimate frame for your chosen proposal. The implication for any would-be influencer at work should be clear. What you compare your idea or proposal with before you present it matters, because what people are exposed to first will have a disproportionate influence over their evaluation of what comes next.

Let's go back to the question posed at the start of Part 2. What advice did you give to your excited, job-seeking friend who called asking about the ideal time, among four shortlisted candidates, to be interviewed?

Before providing an answer, consider the plight of another of my Columbia Business School colleagues, Adam Galinsky.

After completing his PhD studies, Galinsky applied for a job at the University of Chicago. As he was living in New York, the selection committee offered him a choice of interview times. He could travel to Chicago the night before and be the first candidate on the day of the interviews. Alternatively, they could schedule an interview for the afternoon, so he could make the trip in a single day. Not wanting to leave anything to chance, Galinsky sought advice from his Princeton colleagues. Unanimously they advised: "Go first!"

There are good reasons why this is sound advice. Research from the 1960s and 1970s demonstrates how, after reviewing a list of words, people tend to remember those presented either at the beginning or towards the end of the list. Interestingly, when there is a time delay between the review of the list and recalling it later, people are more likely to remember the words that appeared at the beginning rather than the end.[8] Maybe that's why Galinsky's colleagues advised him to choose to be interviewed first. So he did. The interview went well. A few days later he was contacted by the recruitment board with some news. He didn't get the job.

To suggest he didn't get the job because he was the first to be interviewed is silly. More likely another candidate performed better on the day. But the experience gnawed away at Galinsky, prompting him to delve deeper into whether the order in which candidates are interviewed has any influence on recruitment decisions. He started with the hiring records at Princeton University and found something remarkable: with a few exceptions, candidates who were interviewed last were much more likely to get the job. Casting his net further afield he found the last-candidate effect wasn't limited to academic appointments. An analysis of 50 years of results from the *Eurovision Song Contest* found that countries whose singers performed in the latter stages of the competition were typically awarded higher marks than those who performed earlier. The same with *American Idol*. The *X-Factor* too.

Maybe recruiters' memories of early candidates fade, so later candidates have an unfair advantage. Yet research shows this "last-performer advantage" holds true even when candidates are evaluated after each individual performance rather than evaluating them all at the end.

Perhaps a better explanation comes by reviewing these results through the lens of framing effects. It is easy to assume that the first candidate holds an advantage because they set the benchmark by which the others are judged. But this ignores an important point. Recruiters already have a frame of reference. It comes in the form of the job description, a document that typically describes their image of a heaven-sent candidate. That alone might be enough to disadvantage any first candidate. After all, few candidates are likely to possess the skills to match a recruiter's ideal. But they are further weakened by another framing effect. When assessing multiple performances, judges tend to be harsher in the early stages. They may worry that giving high marks to early candidates won't leave them reserves to reward better performers later in the process. Awarding 5/5 to the first candidate during a competency-based interview leaves no room for extra reward should a subsequent candidate perform better. Consequently, early applicants might be at a disadvantage. Not based on the evidence, but on the framing of that evidence.

So if you suggested that your job-seeking friend ask to be interviewed later rather than earlier in the process, they should consider themselves fortunate. Not only do they have someone in their life who is willing to give their advice freely. They also have someone in their life whose advice is wise.

Consider the wider implications. Imagine that the influence challenge you face relates to a competitive situation with multiple entrants, such as gaining a promotion, winning a new account or haggling for your fair share of next year's budget. How might framing, and the timing of your input, affect the desired outcome? All else being equal, arranging for your proposal to appear towards the end of the process might place you at an advantage. That's not to say that candidates seen later in the process always win. In fact, evidence suggests that in situations where there are only two proposals or candidates, the first is more likely to come out on top. Your first job, then, is to know how many entrants you're up against. That will determine your ideal positioning.

In summary, the wise persuader will always ensure they frame their evidence optimally by presenting an appropriate, truthful comparison first. Doing so allows them to maintain control of the context in which that evidence – be it a message, presentation or proposal – is received.

But framing isn't the only way to ensure that the persuasive part of your evidence is optimised. You should also carefully consider a second factor: the person or entity communicating that evidence.

The messenger

Is the message

When doctors at Sutter Health, a California-based health provider, began routinely introducing the expertise of their diabetes nurses to patients in advance of healthcare checks, something interesting happened.[9] Patients were much more likely to attend future appointments, which meant a welcome reduction in costly no-shows for hospitals and clinics. That's not all. These same patients were much more likely to report higher levels of confidence and satisfaction, not just in the nurses who treated them but also in the organisation itself.

The upsides didn't stop there. Being legitimately introduced as "a professional with advanced training and over 10 years' experience" seemed to have an effect on the nurses too. Managers reported that performance rose and absenteeism fell. By giving people pride-boosting, genuine labels of competence, something important seems to happen. People live up to them.

Although it's hard to prove for certain that it was the introductions alone that persuaded patients and carers to change their behaviours, it's unlikely they occurred by chance. That's because the information and advice provided by nurses to patients never changed. What did change was what was said *about* the nurses – *before* any information or advice was presented. The evidence never changed. What changed was people's perception of the messenger delivering that evidence.

Most of us have experienced the frustration of not having our ideas and proposals listened to or taken seriously. It's a frustration that can quickly turn to annoyance when someone else – maybe someone from a different department, an outside consultant or even a competitor – says exactly what we've been saying and suddenly everyone thinks it's the best idea since sliced bread. The fact that nothing about the idea has changed, or that the proposal now being enthusiastically embraced is based on the same evidence as the one roundly rejected a few days previously, barely seems to matter.

This commonplace scenario illustrates something crucial about the use of evidence in the practice of influence. Often it's not the evidence itself that sways audiences' opinions nor how the evidence is framed, but the person or entity delivering it. Any evidence used to inform and influence an audience takes a back seat and is replaced by a feature or characteristic of the person presenting that evidence. The messenger *becomes* the message.

When someone presents evidence and information designed to influence others, something intriguing happens. The persuader becomes connected to the content of that evidence and information in the mind of their audience. This can have a dramatic impact on how they are subsequently perceived by the audience.

This concept goes some way to explaining the origin of the centuries-old phrase "shooting the messenger" where warring generals were apt to punish emissaries who brought bad news from the battlefield. Legend has it that when an envoy arrived to inform Tigranes, King of Armenia, that Roman forces were about to attack, Tigranes responded by promptly chopping off the envoy's head.[10] One assumes that all subsequent news destined for Tigranes's ears was wholly positive (and probably less reliable).

But it's not just centuries-old heads of dynasties who fail to separate the evidence being communicated from the person communicating it. We all do. At work we can probably think of a time when a charismatic colleague was chosen over a more thoughtful one, when an attractive communicator trumped an accurate one, or when the dominant voice in the room overpowered the more discreet and dependable one.

A few years ago, my colleague Joseph Marks and I embarked on a programme of research to understand who, in today's society, is likely to be heard and who is more likely to be ignored. Our work uncovered a range of successful characteristics – eight, in fact – which we published in the book *Messengers*.[11] When it comes to influence at work, three of these characteristics are worthy of particular attention: competence, similarity and trustworthiness.

Competence

Communicators who are perceived to possess competence are more likely to be listened to because they are seen to have the experience, skills and knowledge that can help others to achieve their goals. But a problem arises for any would-be influencer. How do you signal to those you wish to persuade that you *are* competent and worthy of attention? One option – to begin any presentation or proposal by outlining a long list of your qualifications, achievements and successes – seems wholly counter-productive. Such a strategy will likely create, rather than remove, any barriers that might exist between you and your audience. But the strategy is not without merit. The key is to arrange for the expertise and wisdom you do possess to be introduced by someone else. Interestingly, it's an approach that is effective even when the person introducing you stands to gain from any subsequent success.

A few years ago, some colleagues and I conducted a small study in the offices of an independent London-based property sales and letting firm.[12] Like many companies it was struggling to differentiate itself from competitors that offered similar services and at comparable fees. We noticed that the first contact any potential customer had with the firm was typically via a front-of-house receptionist who would field incoming calls and answer website enquires. Having elicited the nature of the enquiry, the receptionist would ensure that leads were quickly channelled to the associate best positioned to help. The process was slick and impressive. But one thing struck us as odd. At no point did the receptionist ever mention their colleagues' competence, expertise or experience.

We proposed a small adjustment to the process, which yielded an immediate 20% increase in the number of enquiries converted into appointments. It also triggered a

15% rise in the number of contracts the firm closed. Before connecting potential customers to a colleague best placed to help, the receptionist was simply instructed to highlight their competence and experience honestly. "Selling your property? Let me connect you to Peter. He is our head of sales and has 20 years of experience selling properties in this area."

It's not only nurses in diabetes clinics and estate agents who can benefit from a thoughtful introduction. We all can. The costless nature of this strategy alone warrants its widespread application. But there are some contexts in the workplace where it is particularly recommended.

One is for people who are early in their careers. Another is people who have recently joined a company and who are seeking to build their influence within it. As I reach the later years of my career, I am increasingly struck by how those who traditionally look like the most knowledgeable and expert in the room, frequently are not. A case in point is my own consultancy. I am lucky to have a team of colleagues who are not only kind and considerate, but also phenomenally clever. It is not unusual for them to attend meetings where they are one of the smartest people – and sometimes the smartest person – in the room. Yet whether they get heard is frequently determined by how they are introduced. When their credentials are introduced, what was otherwise a group of curmudgeonly individuals can hang on their every word. When they aren't, the opposite frequently occurs.

A recommendation emerges that increases the influence of all concerned. Leaders and managers should be alert to opportunities for introducing the legitimate expertise, skills and potential that their colleagues possess. Remember, when doctors started introducing the expertise of their nurses, it wasn't just that patients listened more. Nurses' performance rose too.

One obvious opportunity to do this is at work meetings that start by someone suggesting people go round the table and introduce themselves. A few moments of reflection are all that's needed to conclude how unhelpful a way to start any meeting this is, for several reasons. One concerns the immediate anxiety felt, at least by some people, that they are going to have to talk about themselves in a room full of strangers. Otherwise, why bother with introductions at all? Although there will always be the odd precocious member willing to talk about how their vital and timely contribution on "Project Splendid" pulled victory from the jaws of defeat, self-aggrandising doesn't come naturally for most people. Consequently, they simply affirm what might appear on their email signature.

"Hi. I'm Steve from IT."

It is also worth pointing out that what people say probably doesn't matter anyway, because hardly anyone is listening. Instead, they are mentally rehearsing what they are going to say when it's their turn. Any relevant information from fellow attendees is likely to be missed. And the introductions and insights they themselves make are likely to go unheard too, for the same reason.

There's a simple fix. Whoever is in charge of hosting the meeting, or one of the senior people in the room, should take responsibility for introducing everyone. It neatly sidesteps these problems and is also efficient. The meeting organiser should be able to say something useful about everyone in the room; if they can't, then perhaps that person shouldn't have been invited.

An equally simple fix is available in situations where you need to introduce your expertise but lack someone to speak on your behalf, like one-to-one appointments. Here the recommendation is to arrange for your expertise to be sent out in advance via an introductory email. Along with a welcome note and an agenda include a two-line biography that summarises your expertise and experience. And if your meeting takes place via Zoom or Teams, be sure to include your official title or qualifications beside your name. For example, financial professionals who legitimately included their qualifications (CFP, APFS, etc.) alongside their name during online consultations forced by covid-19 lockdown restrictions reported increased follow-up appointments and referrals from their clients.

And to those early in their careers and keen to build influence: if your manager isn't currently introducing your expertise and know-how before you present, you need to ask them to do so. Or maybe find a manager who will.

Similarity

We're all familiar with the saying "opposites attract". An example might even come to mind. A couple who stand out because of how different they are to each other: she much taller than him, or vice versa. Or he a quiet, reflective type, she a more flamboyant and charismatic character.

"Birds of a feather flock together" is another familiar saying. Examples of this maxim should be far easier to bring to mind because birds of a feather are far more likely to flock together than opposites. It is a fact fundamental to influence. People are typically more inclined to listen to and accept proposals coming from those with whom they share a perceived similarity than those they don't. As well as asking themselves if the evidence they're hearing is coming from a competent messenger they might also ask: "Is the evidence coming from someone who is like me?"

Imagine you have recently received a modest inheritance

and arrange to meet two financial advisers. Jane Brown is competent and has an impressive track record. Yet after meeting her there is something that didn't quite "click" for you on a personal level. But then you meet John Smith. It's like you are peas from the same pod. His investment record is OK but doesn't match Jane's noteworthy returns. Which of them do you choose to invest Aunt Lillian's parting gift?

The objectively correct answer is to follow the evidence and select Jane. But many will instead favour the advice coming from a similar other, even if that similar other has little experience or expertise in the matter.

There's a lesson here that interested influencers need to bear in mind. Even if we are viewed as possessing good evidence and competence, these factors may not be enough to convince everyone. Therefore, before any influence attempt, it is important to arrange not only for your competence to be highlighted but also the genuine similarities shared between you and your audience. This requires preparation. LinkedIn can be a great tool. A few moments invested in identifying commonalities can potentially smooth the way to persuasion. Think shared experiences, similar career trajectories, the same university. And where possible, find the "uncommon commonalities" (things you share that most other people do not) that can build rapport instantly. A shared affinity for Burmese cats, perhaps.

Legitimate expertise and feline harmonies aside, there is a third attribute of the persuasive messenger that is likely to affect how receptive an audience will be to their advice and evidence.

Trustworthiness

Trust is crucial to any human relationship. It is hard to build productive workplace collaborations and prosperous economic exchanges without it. Dr Anna Koczwara is a behavioural scientist and an authority on building trust in business and workplace settings. Koczwara reports that there are two kinds of trust:

- competence-based trust
- integrity-based trust.

The latter is especially important to advancing your influence at work because it signals an intent to uphold moral standards, even when there's an opportunity to violate them to your advantage. This is important when it comes to persuading others with evidence because it's tempting (and easy) to "cherry pick" data, presenting it in a way that supports your case – and only your case. But any short-term success gained doing this can come at a longer-term cost.

Koczwara describes integrity as "the ability to uphold strong, morally accepted principles through repeated contact over time". This seems right, prompting two recommendations. The first is to adopt what influence researchers call the "two-sided argument". These work by acknowledging early on in your proposals and presentations that options other than your own also have advantages. Interestingly, research suggests this approach is particularly effective if you suspect your audience may be resistant, or even hostile, to your proposition.

The other is to foster regular contact with people, especially at times when you do not need to persuade them of anything. Studies show that managers who initiate, maintain and encourage frequent social exchanges are rated not only as more likeable and productive but also considered more trustworthy and, by definition, influential.[13] There's an important lesson here. Token, perfunctory exchanges with others is unlikely to be enough to build trust and influence. Genuine, sustained influence comes through repeated and meaningful interactions. Influence, it would seem, is a contact sport.

The rule of three

Three charms. Four alarms

On the afternoon of November 19th 1863, Edward Everett, a former President of Harvard University and US Secretary of State, mounted the speaker's platform that had been temporarily erected in a cemetery in Gettysburg, Pennsylvania to address the waiting crowd. His 13,607-word speech was scheduled on the day's programme as the "Gettysburg Address".[14] He spoke elegantly and with clarity for more than two hours.

Shortly afterwards, Abraham Lincoln delivered his speech. It was 272 words long and took him two minutes. "The world will little note, nor long remember, what we say here," he predicted. He was wrong about that. His concise, yet profound and uplifting message will forever be remembered.

And Everett's? Not so much.

There are many reasons why Lincoln's speech has endured as one of the most memorable and influential.[15] The context of the American Civil War clearly added a significance and reverence to the address. So did two other features central to this chapter: the framing and the messenger.

Lincoln's speech came after a marathon. His speech wasn't even planned to be the central one of the day. Is it possible that what came before Lincoln's short address potentially elevated it? Maybe. The messenger mattered too. A former Harvard president and Secretary of State would usually top any playbill, but surely not one that also includes the President of the United States?

But a third factor is also worthy of attention, one which almost certainly had an influence. It concerns a question faced by any communicator wishing to construct a persuasive appeal. The question is not "What should be said?" but "How much?"

Readers may have noticed something about the form and composition of this book. To my best effort, I have attempted to structure it around the rule of three: three parts, three motivations, a three-component Influence Equation. And nested within each component, three sub-components. It's not a new idea. *"Omne trium perfectum"* ("Everything that comes in threes is perfect"). Think: *Location, Location, Location*. Stop, look, listen. Sex, drugs, rock 'n' roll. Mind, body, spirit. Lions, tigers and bears. I came, I saw, I conquered.

Humans have a psychological preparedness for things in threes. It begins in the earliest of infant–caregiver interactions. Lullabies and nursery rhymes often come in a numerical three pattern. "Hush Little Baby" soothes the child with the promise of a mockingbird, a diamond ring and a looking glass. The sing-song nursery rhymes passed down through the generations embed themselves in the young brain, lessons learned from stories like "The Three Little Pigs", "Goldilocks and the Three Bears", and "The Three Billy Goats Gruff".

Psychologically, three is key for pattern recognition because it is the smallest number required to create a beginning, middle and end, which is a structure that allows our brain to process information efficiently. From patterns we derive meaning, uncover insight and find order amid chaos. It's a fundamental skill in human cognition to find emerging patterns – and it begins with three.

When it comes to communication and influence in the workplace, the rule of three applies too. Blog writing is an important part of any good brand's content strategy. The "listicle" is perhaps now the most used approach, with three being the go-to number. Along with other odd numbers, lists based on three things tend to get the more clicks and higher engagement on social media. The same goes for professionals in the consulting and services business. McKinsey, a consulting firm, advocates a three-point rule that has been adopted by many advisers when presenting recommendations to busy executive clients. "I've got three reasons why you should do this," is the holy mantra of the McKinsey associate. The insight has a Goldilocks quality when it comes to presenting evidence. Not too much, not too little, just right.

An important insight emerges when it comes to presenting evidence, be it empirical, expert or anecdotal. Less is often more. When the Make-A-Wish charity invited people to donate, its appeal included either two egocentric reasons or two altruistic reasons to give. Both worked similarly well. But when all four reasons were provided on invitations to donate, people gave much less. Follow-up surveys revealed the reason why. The appeal was seen for what it was: an overt appeal to persuade.[16]

Suzanne Shu, a US marketing professor, offers empirical evidence on the appropriate amount of evidence to support a case persuasively.[17] She presented information to people about a range of products, premises and people including breakfast cereal, shampoo, a restaurant, an ice cream parlour and a politician. In each case the pitch was accompanied by one, two, three, four, five or six pieces of supporting evidence. Attitudes to each were then rated, including measuring levels of doubt and scepticism about the claims. Whether about breakfast cereals, restaurants, politicians or shampoos, one approach emerged head and shoulders above the rest. Those exposed to two or three proof points or messages rated the appeals significantly more positively than those exposed to one, four, five or six. Adding additional claims only increased persuasion up to the third one listed. After that cynicism increased, which led to resistance to the claim or evidence being presented.

There is no doubt that evidence is a crucial component of any influence appeal – hence its inclusion in the Influence Equation. Often though it's not the evidence itself that influences the outcome, but how it is presented. Framing evidence optimally by presenting a comparison is crucial. So is ensuring that you don't just attend to the message but also give careful thought to who is the optimal messenger to deliver the message. Finally, be alert to how much evidence you present. The master influencer engages their audience with evidence and doesn't overwhelm them.

Remember: three charms, but four alarms.

5

Influencing with economics

On the second day of our Executive Education programme at Columbia Business School, my colleague Stephan Meier – an economics professor and expert on the future of work – leads a session on incentives and the role they play in influencing behaviour. I like Stephan a great deal. Everyone does. He is smart and engaging with a sharp wit. He can be a little mischievous too.

He will often begin a talk by challenging the class to think about ways to address a common problem without resorting to a financial incentive. One test concerns supermarket shopping trolleys. Some customers fail to return them to designated areas after using them, instead abandoning them before driving off. Untidy car parks, pedestrian hazards and costly scratches to paintwork can result. In some cases, trolleys end up on streets and pavements, which has both social and environmental impacts. Some trolleys have even been found in rivers and at popular fly-tipping spots.

Keen to impress their professor, the class gets to work proposing an array of creative solutions. Increased use of CCTV. A social disapproval campaign where photos of serial offenders are posted on in-store screens and notice boards. A trolley hotline for conscientious shoppers to report sightings of discarded shopping trolleys so that collection squads can retrieve them. Geo-enabled tags that cause trolley wheels to lock should it go beyond the supermarket's car park. Some people have even suggested giving the trolleys names; maybe shoppers would be less likely to abandon their trolley after learning it's called Tommy or Tina.

After patiently listening to the responses, Meier commends the group's ideas before gently dismissing them with a knowing smile. Demanding the issue be addressed without the use of a financial incentive is, he observes, a fool's errand. The problem is easily solved with basic economics. Simply attach a deposit device to trolleys that requires shoppers to insert a coin to release it and that they only get back after returning it to a designated area.

It's a beautiful solution. And one central to classic economic thinking. If you want to persuade someone to do something, give them an incentive. And if you want to persuade someone not to do something, introduce a cost or a penalty.[1]

Economic incentives are wonderfully effective and a crucial tool for anyone interested in influencing people's decisions, actions and behaviours. Incentives have a near-universal appeal. Everyone understands them. They are mostly easy to implement, and they apply to all manner of contexts, not just wayward shopping trolleys.

Consider voting. In the United States and the UK, the percentage of voter turnout in general elections ranges from the mid-40s to the mid-60s. It is considerably lower in local and state elections. How can a society persuade more of its citizens to undertake this socially desirable act and turn out to vote? Why not just pay them? This is not as an absurd idea as it might first seem. According to the country's Electoral Commission, voter turnout in Australian General Elections is never less than 90%. Dodgy dictatorships aside, it is one of the highest rates in the world. There's a simple reason why. Since 1924, voting in Australia has been compulsory. If you fail to cast your vote on election day you are fined.[2]

A clear lesson from Meier's lecture emerges. If you want to influence people's behaviours, there's a solution. Use an economic incentive.

Class dismissed.

*

Of course, even the most belligerent of economists – which Meier is most definitely not – will acknowledge that life isn't so straightforward. Yes, people respond to incentives; no question about that. What is also without question is how people's responses to incentives are shaped by context and psychological mechanisms. For example, imagine you are asked to choose between receiving £20 today or waiting a day and receiving £21 tomorrow. Most people choose to take the cash today. Now consider this choice. Would you prefer £20 in seven days' time or £21 in eight days' time? When presented with this option, more people elect to wait an extra day, despite the delay being the same in both cases.[3]

Economics, particularly in the form of incentives, are an important ingredient in any successful influence strategy. Also important are the largely predictable ways in which people respond to them. Consequently, economic incentives offer would-be persuaders numerous ways to frame and present offers in a way that makes their ideas and proposals more compelling. That's not to say that the amount at stake – whether a price, a reward or a bonus – doesn't matter. It matters a lot. If the product, idea or proposal you're peddling is similar to that of a competitor but yours is priced higher, you might struggle to convince your client, customer or colleague. Even if your offer or idea is priced similarly, other factors will matter too – like availability, ease of use and the perceived attractiveness of what you are offering. But let's assume you have a good financial case to argue – one where the economics and finances stack up. (Again, if you don't, then fix this first.) This chapter explores reliable ways to present and frame economic incentives that can exert a heavy influence on people's acceptance of your idea or proposal.

Specifically, I focus on three persuasive ways to present economic incentives without having to change the price or amount on offer. But before diving in, we should briefly review what we mean by economic incentives and describe some of the common types of incentives available to you when influencing others.

What are incentives?

Simply put, incentives are rewards designed to influence a person or people to make a decision, undertake an action, or both. They are fundamental to economics and, consequently, to persuading others, especially in business and workplace environments where, unlike family and personal situations, the motivation to act is less likely to be driven by familial obligations and social connections. Economic incentives are built on a simple premise: people respond to and are more likely to undertake an action when they stand to gain something. And they are more inclined to avoid an action or situation when they are exposed to a risk or loss.

Broadly, economic incentives fall into one of two categories.[4]

Financial incentives include monetary items like remuneration, bonuses, share options and commissions.

Non-financial incentives comprise rewards that, although not providing an immediate monetary boost, are nonetheless valuable. In the workplace these include on-the-job training, career development opportunities, well-being programmes or simply recognition for a job well done.

Similar to influencing through the use of evidence, when it comes to influencing people using economic incentives, it is often not the incentive itself that sways a decision but the way in which those incentives are presented or framed. There are three things that those wishing to be more influential should consider when crafting their appeals.

1. When to offer incentives: frequency and timing.
2. How to frame incentives: gains and losses.
3. Who identifies with the incentives: the importance of ownership.

Frequency and timing

Present pennies versus distant pounds

With more than 75 million records sold, Reba McEntire is adored by American country music fans. And bus drivers. At the end of her concerts the Oklahoma singer, known simply as Reba to worshipping fans, first praises the talents of the musicians with whom she has shared a stage. She then thanks the drivers who ferry her and her band between venues.

"Finding a good bus driver is as important as finding a good musician," Reba proclaims.

Alex Guariento, a 30-year veteran of the public transportation industry, would no doubt agree. For decades his goal has been to ensure that the buses, coaches and trucks under his supervision reach their destination not only on time, but also safely and without incident. It's easier said than done.

From the perspective of the passengers who travel on buses and coaches, things should be straightforward. The drivers who transport them to and from work and home, an airport terminal or on a tour require only a limited skillset: an operational knowledge of the vehicle they are driving and the competence to do so safely. Things like a friendly demeanour and the occasional smile, although welcome, are usually viewed as icing on the cake.

For the drivers themselves, however, the job is anything but straightforward. Professional drivers spend many more hours on the road than the average motorist. As a result, they are at an increased risk of being involved in an incident or collision. Crash causation studies find as many as one in ten non-fatal crashes involves a driving professional operating a large vehicle or bus. (A bus is defined as having at least nine seats.) Include fatal crashes and the figure rises to one in eight cases.[5]

Furthermore, driving for long periods is boring and complex. Seemingly easy tasks like staying in the right lane and following familiar routes become automatic and mindless. Distractions from noisy, irritated passengers can add to the challenge. So do unexpected events like a car in front braking suddenly, cyclists slaloming between vehicles and pedestrians stepping into bus lanes, faces glued to smartphones. Some people in the industry claim that driving a bus is more cognitively draining than flying a commercial airliner. Given the auto-pilot capabilities of modern aircraft and the fact there are dual operators, they may have a point.

When it comes to encouraging safe driving practices the industry has a widely accepted rule of thumb. Dubbed the "two-second rule", it advocates drivers ideally allow a two-second gap between their moving vehicle and the one in front.[6] The rule is based on reaction times rather than stopping distances and has been reliably shown to reduce collisions and minimise heavy braking, both of which can result in costly litigation. But, as Alex Guariento and other transport managers know only too well, what is advised and what is actually done are not always the same. The challenge for Guariento is to persuade bus drivers to follow the rule.

Economic incentives can help. Interestingly, Guariento finds that it is not the incentive itself that improves outcomes but their timing and frequency. He notes how bus drivers offered a monthly bonus ($100 a month) for adhering to the two-second following rule are much less likely to achieve it consistently than drivers who are paid the same amount but more frequently ($25 per week).[7] This change highlights an important insight for anyone using incentives to influence behaviour. Offering smaller and more immediate (i.e. frequent) incentives will often trump larger, less frequent ones.

Why? Because increasing the frequency of bonuses provides a much more immediate and salient feedback mechanism even if the amount itself remains the same. Incentives work by providing a signal between an action and a reward. They act as a reinforcer to a desired action or behaviour. And if these reinforcements are repeated enough over time, they might create useful new routines or habits.[8]

Savvy managers realise this. That's why it can be effective to offer commissions to sales teams and customer service staff on each sale or new customer win, rather than offering a larger carrot over a longer period (like an annual bonus). Organisations keen to attract and retain customers recognise this too. Banks, credit institutions and suppliers of finance products will often offer smaller, more frequent bonuses in the form of loyalty points and cashback. It's a strategy that can be especially effective in the early months of a newly opened account where the desire to build customer loyalty quickly is prized. Once the connection between a desirable behaviour and reward is made, our brains, in true Pavlovian style, will often take care of the rest.

Research shows how smaller, more frequent incentives are often more effective when attempting to influence the achievement of short-term goals and objectives, like finding a new client or encouraging a restaurant owner to provide good customer service.[9] Or, as in the case of Guariento and his transport company, persuading drivers to be vigilant on their next shift.

Smaller, more frequent incentives can also work on a much larger scale. In the late 2000s, a financial crisis brought the world economy to its knees. Policymakers in the US Treasury, charged with stimulating spending in response to the resultant recession, implemented a tax-rebate programme with a difference. Rather than provide one-off payments, tax refunds were distributed in smaller amounts over a period of months with citizens receiving the extra cash in their monthly pay cheques. The strategy worked. Instead of choosing to deposit a single larger amount in a savings account or their pension pot, those receiving the smaller, more frequent payments were more likely to respond to this boost in their disposable income by spending a little more.

It is a useful insight for anyone interested in influencing the actions of others. People and societies seem increasingly focused on the present and might struggle to appreciate distant rewards. So rather than offering larger, delayed economic incentives, dividing them into more proximal and immediately gratifying incentives can be helpful. Even when the overall amount is the same, or – as in the case of waiting for a £21 versus a £20 reward – less.

Paying per unit

Dividing a large incentive into smaller parts can be an effective way to persuade people. A similar concept can be applied when attempting to persuade people to accept propositions and proposals that come at a price. For example, research has shown how audiences are often more willing to accept a larger proposal, if they first consider the price of a smaller part of that proposition. The approach is called *unit asking*.[10]

Here's an example. Imagine that you run a charity that supports people in need. You have noticed how regular donors typically have a "default" amount they give which, once set, is hard to shift. What might you do to persuade these donors to increase the amount of money they usually give? Studies conducted by Christopher Hsee, a behavioural economist at the University of Chicago, show that a unit-asking strategy can spark a healthy increase in contributions. Here's how. Rather than ask for a contribution that will go towards helping a group of vulnerable people, potential donors are first asked how much they think a single person within that group might need. In one of Hsee' s studies, donors who were first asked to consider the needs of a single student from an impoverished family gave almost twice as much to the appeal as those who were simply asked to contribute to the campaign.

In addition to fundraising and charitable appeals, there are other areas where a unit-asking approach might lead to favourable outcomes. Take, for example, an activity that many of us at work find both necessary and daunting: negotiating for budget and resources. When seeking an increase in their annual travel budget, managers might be more successful if, before asking for their desired amount, they first ask purse-holders to think about the cost of a single trip. School governors and teachers lobbying parents for money towards schoolbooks and sports equipment could ask mums and dads to estimate the cost of meeting the needs of one child before asking them to donate on behalf of the whole classroom. A hobbyist might attract higher bids for his or her collection of treasured possessions on an online marketplace if they ask: "How much would you be willing to pay for just one Beenie baby (or this retro pair of shoes?)" rather than posting a reserve price for the lot. Even financial advisers, who often face the challenge of persuading people to save more for the future, might find a client increases the amount they routinely deposit in pensions and savings accounts investments, if they first focus their client's attention on the increasing cost of regularly purchased items, like a weekly food shop, their monthly utilities bill or an annual holiday.

The same logic is a useful tactic for savvy auctioneers. When selling off a collection of items, say vintage wines, the auctioneer could apply the unit-asking method by first prompting potential bidders to consider the value of a single bottle in the collection before bidding on the lot. Once bidders establish a value anchor based on one single bottle, they may well increase their perceived value of the entire collection by mentally multiplying the single unit value across the whole collection. The potential result? Higher bids across the board.

One reason why the unit-asking technique can be effective is because it mirrors what many people who are thinking about costs and prices do naturally anyway. Many of us naturally tend to separate large amounts into smaller units. Classic economists posit that all money is interchangeable. Behavioural economists and psychologists do not. Take, for example, the concept of "mental accounting" – a term coined by Nobel laureate Richard Thaler – which describes the inclination to divide up our money into different mental "pots". Think rent, food, entertainment, travel and savings. This can make the task of influencing tough because people are often reluctant to transfer funds between these mental pots. Persuading a friend to go the cinema becomes harder if they have to spend money from their "clothing" pot. Similarly, in the workplace, it can be tough convincing a manager to fund a training course you want to attend if it requires them to use funds from another budget pot. It's not that the money isn't available; it's just that it resides in a differently labelled mental pot.[11]

Another factor is how these mental pots become depleted over time. People tend to think and feel more negatively about a proposition to the extent that it strains or exhausts what is left of their budget. A product purchased when mental pots are full is less painful than the same product purchased when mental monetary tanks are empty. This is called the "bottom-dollar effect". The bottom line (*sorry*) for the bottom-dollar effect is a simple one. Regardless of the cost of your idea or proposal, people's view of it will be influenced by whether you make your offer at the start or end of their allocated mental budget. Money spent at the beginning of a budget period when mental pots are full will be much less psychologically painful to the spender than the same decision made when monetary tanks are drained. A £50,000 ($65,000) training programme spent from a budget of £1m represents just 5% of the total. But later in the year, when only £100,000 remains, that same £50,000 now represents half the budget. The amount hasn't changed, but the reference point has, which puts a different perspective on the same thing.[12]

It also explains why savvy supermarkets offer "Buy one, get one free" incentives from the middle and towards the end of the month. Assuming that most people are paid at the end of each month, it ensures that customers feel better by helping to diminish any negative feelings associated with spending money.

Skilled operators remember this and recognise that their persuasive prowess is often not so much a function of the right price or incentive but the right timing – even for activities that don't require spending money. Banks who remind consumers that a "change in season should prompt a change in saving" often experience a boost in new deposit accounts. Dating apps register upticks in engagement when they remind users that "a new month could spark a new love". Even healthcare providers are getting in on the act with text messages to those about to enter a new decade: "Now you're 40 ... get that check-up!"

Present pennies or distant pounds?

The fast-paced and present-oriented nature of modern life, where gratification of the now can crowd out a consideration of tomorrow, might lead us to suppose that splitting economic incentives into smaller and more timely bonuses is always best. But given how complex human behaviour can be and how dependent it is on the context; this would be a mistake. Larger, longer-term incentives – like annual bonuses and stock options – play a crucial role too, particularly when the projects and tasks you are encouraging others to undertake are multifaceted and complicated, and when it's important to discourage risky actions that, although delivering immediate outcomes, might produce unintended and detrimental consequences. It's fine to offer small and frequent rewards to sales staff for each new account won, but incentivising your builder by paying him one brick at a time almost certainly isn't.

The timing and frequency of incentives are crucial factors in determining their effective influence on outcomes. Typically, more frequent and immediate rewards are best deployed when seeking to influence shorter-term behaviours and achieve nearer-term goals. Larger, delayed economic incentives can sustain motivation for longer-term goals.[13] Note too that these should be seen as general guides rather than hard facts.

Beyond frequency and timing, there are other factors that one should keep front of mind when using economic incentives to influence others. An important one concerns people's response not to what they might gain as a result of moving in your direction, but what they could lose.

Gains and losses

Win some, lose more

Imagine you find a £20 banknote on your way to the office one morning. How happy would you be? After sparing a thought for another's bad luck, you might feel pleased with your good fortune. Now imagine that instead of finding cash on the way to work, you open your wallet and find the £20 note you thought you had is not there. How are you feeling now? Pretty unhappy, right?

Most people are much unhappier at the thought of losing rather than gaining the same thing.[14] This raises an intriguing, and admittedly philosophical, question. Imagine you find £20 one morning only to lose it later that day. Would you be worse off? Economically, of course, there would be no difference. Chances are, however, that you would feel psychologically worse off – for the well-established reason that losses loom much larger in our minds than gains. Put another way, losses tend to hijack our attention. The result? Loss becomes a potentially potent tool of influence.

A study by researchers in Australia provides a good demonstration.[15] Householders were provided with a report outlining a series of simple changes they could make to reduce their domestic energy consumption and consequently their bills. Insulating the loft, installing a meter, replacing standard light bulbs with more energy-efficient ones, reducing thermostat settings by a degree or two. That sort of thing.

The researchers were also aware that people, when surveyed, frequently reported their preference for information about ways to save money and make efficiencies. So, included in each report was an estimate of how much money a typical household could reasonably be expected to save as a result of making these changes. For the sake of illustration, let's imagine the figure is £50 ($65) a month. Over the course of a year that's £600 ($750) – a pretty healthy economic incentive. The results of the study found that one group of householders in particular were likely to be persuaded to change. Was it the poorest families struggling to manage a shoestring budget? Or maybe the households who identified as environmentally conscious and already committed to reducing their energy consumption?

No!

The households most likely to change were those who had received a letter informing them they could lose £600 a year if they failed to act. In contrast, those told they could save £600 a year were much less likely to change. The fact that more than twice as many households acted when informed of what they could lose than those who were informed of what they could save, underlines a crucial insight for anyone tasked with influencing others. Loss language can be persuasive and inspire action.

It is over 50 years since psychologists Daniel Kahneman and Amos Tversky published their "prospect theory" which contributed to Kahneman being awarded the Nobel Prize in Economic Sciences.[16] The pair observed that people are typically about twice as motivated to avoid losses than to pursue a comparable gain. This goes some way to explaining why householders in the home energy study were swayed more by the loss message than by the saving one. The concept of loss aversion is reliable and well established. Citations (the number of references made by other researchers to scholarly work) are frequently used as an indication of the worth of scientific research. A publication with several hundred citations usually warrants a place in the top 10% of credible work for a particular discipline. Kahneman and Tversky's paper has almost 80,000. Not only is the loss-aversion finding one of the most quoted in the social scientific literature; it is also one of the most robust. It's no surprise, therefore, how honestly pointing out to colleagues, clients, customers and consumers what they might lose if they fail to follow your advice or recommendation can be a potent influence strategy. But as effective as this approach might be, it is not without its challenges for at least two reasons.

One concerns something most people seem intuitively aware of. When receiving a message, audiences typically prefer positively framed information, which communicates what they might gain and how they could benefit should they accept the idea, recommendation or advice being presented. They typically prefer less of any information conveying what they might lose or that could be to their detriment, even though the latter message is more likely to influence their decisions and actions.[17]

Also, messages frequently become wedded to the messengers who deliver them. As a result, audiences might be more inclined to "like" more those messengers who present rosier pictures and "like" less those who portray gloomier ones. This presents the influencer with a dilemma. The persuasive upsides of presenting what their target stands to lose comes with an unwelcome downside: a risk that they pay a social cost for doing so.

Fortunately, there are mitigations that can help. One concerns *readying* an audience to receive a loss message. It works like this. Before communicating their message, the influence master will acknowledge the potential negative reaction their message might trigger. This forewarning often results in an individual or a group bolstering themselves for what is about to come. And although not guaranteed, empathetically tipping off a target immediately before delivering an emotionally charged message could reduce the potential for a messenger to be shot.

Another important mitigation is to ensure that loss messages are accompanied by a specific action that an audience can take promptly to avoid that loss. In an attempt to increase awareness and boost the vaccination rates for tetanus (a potentially life-threatening condition of the nervous system caused by a toxin-producing bacterium), health campaigners showed graphic images of its consequences on leaflets and billboards. The only thing the campaign seemed to boost successfully was anxiety. But when the campaign was revised to include specific instructions for how and where to get a vaccine, immunisation rates increased significantly.[18] It is a good demonstration of how people are less inclined to deny the personal relevance of a loss-framed message or, worse still, shoot the messenger, when the message comes with an implementable (and ideally easy) action to avoid any risk.

Finally, when using loss-framed messages to persuade others, it is important to communicate the potential losses of something your audience already possesses. I'm not suggesting that it's effective to ask people to imagine losing something they don't currently own, or that is far off in the future – a staple of financial advisers and climate campaigners. It can work sometimes. But its impact is unlikely to be felt as intensely as an actual loss. Imagining losing £20 on the way to work feels very different to actually losing £20 on the way to work. The latter exerts a much greater persuasive punch.

Making losses salient is one likely reason why Brexit's "Leave" campaign – a political and ultimately polarising fight designed to persuade UK citizens to seek a divorce from the European Union – was so effective at mobilising supporters. Politics and points of view aside, campaigners did a pretty good job of highlighting a salient loss: the now-debunked claim that the UK was sending (aka losing) £350 million a week to the EU. The message was clear. This is your money. It is money your NHS is losing out on. Stop this loss. Vote Leave.

In June 2016, 52% of eligible voters in the country did.

That people are more inclined to take action to avoid current, concrete losses over distant and less tangible ones raises an interesting question about the way economic incentives and bonuses are deployed in the workplace. If people are more driven to avoid losses than make gains, surely it would make sense to pay people bonuses in advance? With the money no longer a distant dream but actually in their possession, would people perform duties more diligently in order to keep it?

John List, a US economist, provides evidence to support this idea.[19] Partnering with a Chinese manufacturer of high-tech components and widgets, he found that offering production-line workers an economic incentive in the form of a monetary bonus works pretty well. The productivity of those offered the incentive upfront was almost 2% higher than those promised the bonus at the end. What's more, the effect didn't seem to decline over time. It was a crucial insight that caught the eye of transport chief Alex Guariento.

Earlier in this chapter I described our studies with New York state bus drivers, demonstrating how they were more likely to adhere to recommended safe following distances when they were offered a $25 incentive paid weekly than when they were given a $100 incentive paid monthly. But over time the effect diminished. Four months after instigating the weekly-paid rather than monthly-paid incentive, the difference between the driver groups was indistinguishable.[20] Although disheartened, we took inspiration from List's findings on Chinese production lines and arranged for another group of drivers to be awarded the incentive upfront at the start of each week or month, rather than having to wait. Importantly, the incentive didn't come in the form of cash. Few want to be the person tasked with demanding that New York bus drivers return money paid to them that they didn't qualify for. Instead, the award was made in the form of a future money order. It was tangible and owned – and was something that could be lost. It led to the best outcome for all concerned. The two-second rule was complied with more often, safe driving practices persisted over time leading to less heavy braking incidents, fewer accidents, safer passengers, happier transport managers and better remunerated drivers.

Reba, no doubt, would be proud.

Change is a loss

Losses loom larger in minds than gains – by about twice as much. It's as if our brains have an exchange rate not unlike a foreign conversion counter at an airport. The only difference is that instead of exchanging pounds and dollars, our minds exchange losses and gains – at a rate of 2:1. Anyone seeking to influence others to change should remember this because persuasion often requires us not only to convince an audience to adopt our proposal or proposition, but also to give up something they are currently doing. These two things will not necessarily be valued equally.

In 2013, as part of ongoing austerity reforms by the UK's coalition government, a child tax credit was abolished for higher-rate taxpayers. In an attempt to soften the blow, the Treasury made available childcare vouchers worth around £1,200 a year – about the same as the tax loss – for certain families. The spreadsheets of financial policymakers no doubt reported parity: the loss of £1,200 cancelled out by an equivalent amount in vouchers allocated leaves a net zero. But the exchequer's bloodless maths didn't account for humanity's exchange rate between losses and gains. If people experience losses twice as heavily as gains, then a £1,200 loss might feel more like £2,400. For many, the counter-offer of a £1,200 voucher only met half this psychological loss. The resulting PR disaster faced by the government appeared to confirm this.

The case serves an important reminder to anyone interested in changing the behaviour of others. When seeking to persuade an individual or a group to give up something and take up something else – a company to change from one IT provider to another; a household to convert from a gas boiler to a heat pump; or a doctor to switch from a prescribing an older, familiar pill to a new drug – we need to be alert to how present situations and future states can have different values. When making a case for change, it is important we remember that what people give up in order to move in our direction will be experienced as a loss. This means that making a case based on a small gain or a slight improvement may not be enough. In some circumstances, our proposition might need to be twice as compelling to have a chance of being considered.

The importance of ownership

Value goes, where effort grows

One important reason why economic incentives framed as losses can leverage greater influence concerns the persuasive pull of ownership. Behavioural economists have long known that people assign greater value to things they own or are complicit in creating, than to things that they neither own nor have helped to create.[21]

Termed *endowment*, here's an illustration that readers with a mischievous frame of mind might like to try. Pop down to your local newsagent or corner shop and look out for someone buying a lottery ticket. After witnessing the transaction, approach them and ask if they would be willing to sell it to you. Many aren't. Those who are, are likely to want much more money than they paid only a few moments previously.

The value of the ticket hasn't changed at all, of course. But convincing the owner of this logic is likely to be a lost cause. From their perspective its value is no longer based on any objective market price. Nor is it a simple lottery ticket anymore. It's morphed, albeit only in their minds, to an entirely different kind of ticket. One to a potential new lifestyle of country houses, exotic holidays, fast cars or an ocean-fronted retirement pad.

Similar overvaluations occur when people invest effort into pursuits and endeavours. Mike Norton, a Harvard University professor, calls this the "IKEA effect".[22] His studies demonstrate that people will value a piece of self-assembly furniture they have put together themselves as much as 60% higher than the same furniture assembled by someone else – even the furniture store's resident expert. Our tendency to overvalue things we have purchased or invested effort in appears universal. And it doesn't only happen in our personal lives; it happens at work too. Why?

When it comes to lottery tickets and furniture, the reason seems obvious. We derive pleasure from them; the dream of riches beyond our wildest imagination or a nicely kitted-out crib is agreeable. The thought of losing these pleasures is painful and, therefore, to be avoided. But that's not necessarily the case when it comes to work. Paul Dolan, a professor of behavioural science at the London School of Economics, finds many people rate their job among their least pleasurable activities. But he also points out that unpleasurable is not the same as unrewarding. As challenging and tough as work can be, it doesn't mean it's not satisfying or fulfilling.[23] It appears that people justify the effort they are prepared to expend at work in proportion with the sense of ownership they feel. As ownership of a project increases, so does their likely effort. And as efforts increase, so does their value of how much their project is worth.

This presents a potential boon to managers and supervisors wanting to engage workers better. Many of us know of colleagues who, when briefed on a new idea, project or initiative, adopt a "not invented here" mindset. To counter this, the influence master, rather than issuing commands at the beginning of projects, instead seeks collaboration. They solicit the input and contributions of everyone involved in a programme, especially those minded to play devil's advocate. In addition to elevating the sense of agency and autonomy for the work, the collaborative approach delivers another upside: ownership. And with ownership comes the tendency to increase the perceived worth of an initiative because it *is* their idea. Although I wouldn't claim this is a sure-fire way to convert the whole belligerent, curmudgeonly "not-invented here" brigade, it can be useful, especially in projects and programmes where different departments, and even different suppliers and partners, need to collaborate to deliver a project.[24]

The importance of aligning incentives

Bent Flyvbjerg, an economic geographer at the University of Oxford and author of *How Big Things Get Done*,[25] has spent a career cataloguing major infrastructure projects to determine those that are completed on time and within budget.[26] It makes for dismal reading. He finds that the vast majority of megaprojects – those with a value of at least $1bn – don't meet planned budgets or deadlines.

Examples abound. The Channel Tunnel (an undersea railway tunnel connecting the UK with mainland France) cost 80% more than originally planned. Holyrood (Scotland's parliament building) was competed years late and a colossal 900% over budget. Berlin's Brandenburg Airport opened in October 2020 – nine years late – having missed no fewer than six deadlines. The overspend on the project was so large it inspired a games manufacturer to create a popular board game, the winner being the player who manages to "waste" the most public money.

According to Flyvbjerg, less than one in ten major projects are completed on time and within budget. What makes the successful ones stand out? In addition to a predictable list of attributes like having a clear goal, a common understanding, strong leadership and world-class project management, another feature seems important: a shared incentive that all concerned are motivated to gain rather than lose.

It can work. On March 27th 2008, London Heathrow Airport opened its fifth terminal. T5, as it is now commonly known, was completed on time and within the pencilled £4.3bn budget. A contributing feature of this on-time delivery was an incentive scheme that contractors and their suppliers were enrolled in on the day they broke ground, and that they split equally and immediately after an on-time and on-budget delivery.

Persuading disparate groups to cooperate is challenging

even in the smallest of pursuits. To do so in the context of what was, at the time, Europe's largest building site, is impressive. It is also instructive for those of us charged with influencing others at work. Regardless of how large or small projects are, mobilising teams behind a common goal and making available an economic incentive that align interests and marshals a unifying purpose seems preferable to individual reward-seeking and the invariably costly project creep that frequently follows.

Unintended consequences

In attempt to encourage its citizens to address a shortage in supplies by giving blood, policymakers in Angelholm (a municipality on Sweden's east coast) came up with a novel incentive. Free booze for donors. It worked, but not as intended. Those most willing to roll up their sleeves were heavy drinkers, more interested in helping themselves than others. The idea was quickly withdrawn.

To address a worrying rise in human encounters with venomous cobras, colonial rulers in the city of Delhi offered a bounty for each snake snared and killed. Spotting an opportunity, some of the citizens began breeding cobras in order to slaughter them and claim the cash. When the reward programme was halted, breeders released their snakes into the wild, compounding the problem and increasing the population of lethal reptiles to levels far higher than before.

After introducing a smartphone app that rewarded drivers for driving safely, a US car insurance company recorded an increase in reckless and foolhardy driving. Users discovered that accelerating excessively and then braking abruptly over short periods led to higher scores and reduced premiums. The company had to withdraw the app and rewrite the code.[27]

The importance of economic incentives in influencing people in work and business settings is undeniable. Stephan Meier is right: incentives are wonderful. They are a crucial tool for anyone interested in influencing the decisions, actions and behaviours of others. Everyone understands them. They are (mostly) easy to implement. And universally appealing. Timing and frequency are crucial. Also crucial is the way in which incentives are framed in terms of gains and losses. Ownership is critical, particularly where responsibility for projects is shared and incentives need to be carefully aligned.

But as Swedish blood donors, Indian snake breeders and tricksy drivers show, economic incentives can also be risky, and have unintended consequences. It is important to understand the intricacies of their impact before implementing them widely. Thoughtful design and discrete testing before widespread rollout can help. So can striking the right balance between economic incentives and other factors like intrinsic motivations. People's feelings matter a lot. So much so that emotions also warrant a place on the Influence Equation. And that's what we turn our attention to next.

6

Influencing with emotion

On September 13th 1848, a railway worker laying tracks in the US state of Vermont suffered a horrific accident. An iron rod, over a metre long and used to pack igniting powder into rock, detonated, skewering the man through the left side of his face and passing through his skull with such force that witnesses reported finding the spike 25 metres away. Miraculously, the victim of this accident, Phineas Gage – a 25-year-old foreman working for the Rutland and Burlington Railroad Company – survived.

No one disputes that the event happened. Nor is there any quarrel with reports of Gage's improbable recovery. Within a year he was back at work and, apart from losing the vision in his left eye and some notable scarring, he was observed to be in remarkably good physical health. But as is often the case with narratives from long ago, stories get embellished, memories meander and inaccuracies inevitably creep in. Some say the accident transformed Gage from an otherwise humble, hardworking man into a heavy drinking monster; aggressive, erratic and socially isolated. Others claim the incident limited his future worth to occasional paid-for appearances at Barnum's American Museum in New York. Reports even emerged that, following his death from a seizure in 1860, he was buried with the offending tamping iron because of his unhealthy affection for it. Many claimed hearing him refer to it as his "constant and close companion".[1]

Many of these accounts are dubious. But there is little doubt that the injury would have changed Gage fundamentally. To understand why, we need only turn to modern-day medical science.

Seven years after his death, Gage's body was exhumed to the care of John Martyn Harlow, a physician, who later gave Gage's skull to Harvard Medical School where it remains today. More than a century later, researchers using neuroimaging techniques reconstructed the skull to determine the exact placement of the injury and its likely impact. The findings suggest that Gage suffered injuries to both the left and right prefrontal cortices – a brain region responsible for regulating crucial psychological processes including socio-emotional functioning. The damage, they concluded, would probably have resulted in Gage experiencing problems with emotional processing. Put another way, his judgement and ability to make decisions and regulate his behaviours would have been severely impacted.

Fast feeling

Affect – the term used by psychologists to describe the experiencing of emotion – is rapid, automatic and often bypasses any consideration of the facts. A couple viewing a new house might quickly experience a positive emotional response on stepping through the front door, despite its proximity to a noisy main road. Parents inspecting a school that has only average ratings might be swayed by the warm feeling they experienced with a likeable teacher during their visit. A doctor deciding on a potential treatment for her patient might feel that one drug is the right one to prescribe, despite the availability of a more effective and modern alternative.

Any attention-scarce, overloaded citizen of today, swayed into a decision on the basis of a feeling, would have been roundly dismissed by the philosophers of yesteryear. Emotions are the polluters of reason, they argued. True human intelligence requires an ability to rise above our animal instincts and reptilian ancestry. Acumen and genius, the philosophers would maintain, require judgements and decisions to be made dispassionately with no resort to fervour. Theologians too have typically given emotions a bad rap. The "passions" in Christianity warn of the "seven deadly sins" where emotions such as lust, envy and guilt pull us off the path of righteousness.

Even psychologists, the academics most associated with matters of sentiment, were apt to assign emotions to a back seat. During the cognitive revolution of the 1970s and 1980s, and the emerging neuroscience technologies of the 1990s, emotions were generally considered an afterthought. Plum positions at the most prestigious universities were awarded to those studying the "real" and "hard" cognitive processes that dictated human behaviour. The message seemed clear: emotions weren't considered that important.

Skilled persuaders, however, together with a more recent crop of behavioural scientists, know better. They understand that our feelings about someone or something, and our emotional reactions to stimuli and situations, act as powerful signals exerting a potent influence on our actions and decisions.

This chapter explores how to marshal these feelings and emotional responses to increase your influence. Like in the chapters on evidence and economics, I focus on three important factors to consider when influencing with emotions.

1. Reading and leading the room: mood monitoring and mood making.
2. Selecting the right emotion for the job: emotional fit = message hit.
3. Vehicles of emotions: stories, anecdotes and analogies.

But let's begin by exploring why emotions play such an important role in the practice of influence.

Feelings are data

Traditional economic models of decision-making posit that people make decisions based on the utility of the various choices available to them. After reviewing options, they then calculate the right choice based on factors such as supporting evidence, features and benefits to the decision-maker or user, reliability and, ultimately, price.[2] Proposals deemed to yield the highest expected utility will, according to the theory, win the day. But as Sam and Jake (from the introduction to this book) found to their cost, the reality is different. People's decisions and behaviours are generally limited to the information they are attending to at a given moment, invariably accompanied by an emotional response that might be irrelevant to what is being considered. The perceived warm character of one teacher is hardly representative of a school's quality. But for anxious new parents determining where little Johnny spends his formative years, it is easy to understand how it could be. Emotions, at their core, provide instructive data and feedback. Norbert Schwarz, a psychologist at the University of Southern California, calls this *affect as information*.[3]

Relying on feelings and emotional responses when making a choice or deciding on a course of action can be helpful. There are several reasons why. An obvious one concerns efficiency. In contrast to the laborious process of reviewing various options one after the other, gut feelings offer instant counsel. They can keep us safe too. The intuitive feeling of unease we might experience when meeting a stranger or receiving a text message from an unfamiliar source are helpful alerts to potential risk or danger.

Emotions provide an efficient way to navigate a complex and uncertain world. They allow us to substitute a question that is difficult to answer with an easier one. Parents might replace the hard-to-answer question: "Is this a good school for my children?", with the easier: "How do I feel about this school?" Doctors asking themselves: "What is the best treatment for this patient?" might instead ask themselves: "What feels like the best thing to do?" Often, people just go with their gut feeling.

Going with your gut isn't just a figure of speech. It happens literally. Regions of the brain associated with our emotional responses communicate with the rest of the body, with the resulting bodily sensations signalling to us a possible course of action. Often, we don't "know" the right thing to do as much as much as we "feel" the right thing to do – even in complex decision-making situations.

Or maybe that should read, *especially* in complex decision-making situations.

Antonio Damasio, also from the University of Southern California, calls this process *somatic marker theory*.[4] His work demonstrates how certain bodily sensations –somatic markers – arise, to which the brain attaches a felt emotional experience. We've all experienced this: a rapid heartbeat signals anxiety, an upset stomach can be provoked by disgust. Sometimes it's a nondescript "feeling" that, even though we can't quite put our finger on it, speaks volumes. Damasio's research has shown how these sensations provide instructive information that can improve decision-making. The next time you experience a tightening chest or a turning stomach, here's some advice: listen to your body.

But this is often easier said than done. Personal experience and objective evidence show that our ability to be introspective and reflect on our emotional sensations is a variable skill. Some people have lots of this "interoceptive awareness" or "sixth sense"; others, less so.

Emotions are tricky things. Sometimes they are intense and easily attributable to a particular situation. At other times they are long, drawn-out affairs that gradually merge with other moods and events throughout our day, so we confuse the original source of an emotion – a phenomenon known as *misattribution of arousal*. You might feel frustrated in the afternoon because of an interaction with an annoying colleague earlier in the day but fail to link the two. And after a particularly stressful day at the office, we have all inadvertently taken our anger out on our spouses and the kids. Or the cat.

Such is their importance and impact on decisions and actions that emotions are the third element of the Influence Equation. An awareness of, and their wise use, is crucial for anyone wishing to master the influence process. Three factors are particularly important.

Reading and leading the room
Mood monitoring and mood making

People taking their seats in a US cinema were probably expecting that the film they had chosen to watch would provide a couple of hours of welcome escapism. But Vlad Griskevicius, a psychologist at the University of Michigan, had other ideas. He had devised an intriguing study to demonstrate the powerful impact that an audience's emotional state can have on their decisions and actions.[5]

During the film, Griskevicius arranged for one of two advertisements to be shown, promoting a nearby restaurant. One audience was shown an ad claiming the restaurant to be a popular place, frequented mostly by locals, and often with queues of waiting customers outside, eager to bag a table. The other audience was shown an ad boasting that the restaurant was unique, "one of a kind", and as yet undiscovered by the masses.

Were audiences swayed by these advertisements? They were. But, as Griskevicius had predicted, some audiences were persuaded more by one of the ads, while others were swayed by the other, with the effectiveness of each depending on the specific film they were watching. Those who had chosen the horror movie were much more interested in the restaurant after learning of its popularity. Not so for cinema-goers watching the rom-com. Hearing that lots of people frequented the restaurant had little impact. These folks were more swayed by the uniqueness of the restaurant.

A few moments of reflection should reveal why. Images of a madman slashing his victim with a dagger through a shower curtain will leave most people fearful and on edge. In such a context it's not surprising that a message conveying the presence of many others might be a reassuring one. Being part of a crowd might not entirely eliminate the risk of being singled out by a knife-wielding maniac, but it certainly reduces the odds.

But those watching a film where new love overcomes a seemingly insurmountable set of obstacles and ends "happy ever after" experience entirely different emotions: connection, closeness, intimacy. In this context a bustling, noisy restaurant is less appealing. But an undiscovered, private, one-of-a-kind restaurant? That's much more likely to appeal.

Studies like Griskevicius's offer an important lesson to anyone tasked with persuading others. It is unwise to dismiss the emotional state of the individual or group we are seeking to influence as inconsequential. Masters of the influence process know this and are alert to the emotional state of their audiences, before delivering their message. They are *mood monitors*. They know how the emotional state of a finance director can unduly affect the likelihood that their budget request will be successful and adjust their approach accordingly. They may even bide their time and choose to engage when moods are more amenable to the message they wish to deliver.

But what if it isn't possible to do what the French describe as "smell the air"? Maybe the person you need to influence is someone you are meeting for the first time, and you know little about their current mood. Or maybe you are presenting to a large group who are likely to comprise a melting pot of emotions: some pessimistic, others positive; some cheerful, others despondent. It is in situations like these where the astute influencer takes a different tack: they become the mood maker. Rather than wait for the moment when emotional states are optimal to deliver their message, they take control by eliciting a specific emotion or feeling in their audience favourable to the message they are about to present. Put another way, they prepare their audience emotionally for what they are about to hear. Like a gardener preparing the ground before sowing a crop, they ensure their influence target is readied for what they are about to propose.

But different emotional states serve different purposes eliciting potentially different responses. How do you select the right mood to create?

Selecting the right emotion for the job

Emotional fit = message hit

The range of human emotions is huge. Entire books have been written on single emotional states. Libraries' worth for some of them, like love. But when influencing people at work there is an approach that serves as a useful guide for would-be persuaders who need a steer on which emotion might be most helpful to their cause. Termed the *circumplex grid*, the approach categorises emotions along two dimensions: valence (the relative pleasantness or unpleasantness of the emotion) and arousal (how calming or excitable a reaction the emotion elicits).[6] Figure 4 summarises a range of emotions (in no way exhaustive) that, when experienced, can exert an outsized influence on people's subsequent decisions and actions.

Let's take four of these emotions – anger, disgust, empathy

Figure 4: **The circumplex emotional grid**

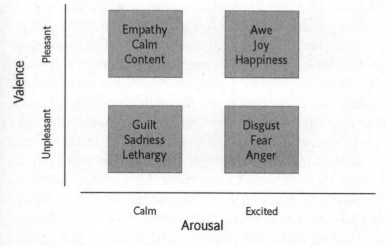

Source: J.A. Russell, "A circumplex model of affect", *Journal of Personality and Social Psychology*, 39(6) (1980), copyright James Russell 1980. Reprinted by kind permission of James Russell

and awe – to demonstrate the influence and impact they can exert on people's decisions and behaviours.

Anger

Most people feel mildly positive most of the time. It is therefore safe to assume that negative moods represent a departure from our usual emotional state. Sadness, for example, is typically triggered by a loss of some kind: the ending of a relationship, the disappointment of an unachieved plan, a promotion not won. Experiencing sadness can expose us to vulnerabilities. Research published in the journal *Psychological Science* suggests that those experiencing low mood are often willing to pay more for the same items as those with an "emotionally neutral" mindset.[7]

Like sadness, anger is also triggered by loss, but the kind of loss where blame can be assigned. We might experience anger when we didn't receive the recognition that a job well done warranted and direct our annoyance at the boss. A competitive colleague might experience anger on learning that they didn't win a prestigious new client account. Rather than acknowledge their own culpability, they attribute the blame to marketing or finance. We can experience momentary anger in response to a less-than-considerate driver, prompting a hand signal or mouthed profanity unlikely to be found in any Highway Code.

Both anger and sadness are experienced as a result of a loss, but the influence of these emotions differs in terms of our subsequent judgement. Although feelings of sadness might lead some unthinkingly to pay more for an item, a much broader body of research finds that sadness is more likely to lead to a greater level of elaboration (thinking). Indeed, research finds that those experiencing a sad or low mood are much less likely to be persuaded by weak arguments.[8]

Convincing the boss that everyone else got it wrong and he really should support your idea for a new cryptocurrency is already a tough sell. And one you should certainly avoid when he is in a gloomy mood.

Not so with anger. The Harvard psychologist Jennifer Lerner shows that our rational thinking becomes much more skewed when we experience anger.[9] Anger propels us. We prioritise short-term gains, and may pay the price in long-term consequences. We act quicker, respond faster. Tempers might fly. Some people even start wars.

Reactionary resentments and hot-headed hostilities aside, it is important to note that the emotion of anger is not always destructive. Marshalled thoughtfully and with restraint, it can be useful. A commercial director seeking to boost sales activity might describe the collective anger his team feels when a lesser competitor is winning their customers. The anger felt by someone witnessing bullying at work or learning of a mindless attack on an innocent citizen might persuade more victims to speak up for the vulnerable, if that person voices their anger.

Disgust

Imagine you are tasked with creating a campaign designed to promote good hygiene in rural African communities. Your client, a team of public health officials, has undertaken lots of research and concluded that persuading people to wash their hands more frequently with soap and sanitiser will do much to reduce gastro-intestinal conditions and other transmitted diseases. As you think about the problem and start to consider a strategy, you might conclude the likely answer lies in improved education and public health awareness. Hundreds of campaigns follow a similar path: educate and create awareness about the problem, promote the benefits of good hygiene, and the desired actions will naturally follow.

Sometimes educational and awareness strategies work. But often they fail because an emotional connection is missing. Disgust, in particular, provides a visceral reaction that can prove effective.

Rather than promoting hand soap and detergents alone, researchers working in Ghana instead focused attention – using a series of short advertisements – on creating a link between disgust and those who failed to wash their hands before touching food, after visiting the toilet. The results were impressive. Before the study, data suggested that barely one in twenty washed their hands with soap after visiting a toilet. This proportion rose considerably after the introduction of emotional disgust. Soap use rose and four in ten reported washing their hands with soap before eating.[10] Research has found messages that provoke feelings of disgust can improve hygiene behaviours in western societies too.

Disgust influences our behaviour because of its close links to our survival. Evolutionary psychologists have shown that feelings of disgust played a central role in our predecessors' choices about what to eat, where to live and who to interact with. Modern-day societies are by no less immune to the influence of disgust, although these days it is just as likely to be employed for the purposes of entertainment as for existence. Anyone who has witnessed a minor celebrity or chastened politician eating camel penis on reality television knows exactly what I'm talking about.

The US psychologist Jonathan Haidt has demonstrated how disgust and anger can combine to wield a strong influence on our sense of right and wrong.[11] When carefully marshalled, this brace of emotions can spark indignation, a desire for justice and can potentially reduce antisocial and other undesirable behaviours. My own work, carried out with my colleagues Joseph Marks and Alice Soriano, provides a telling example. In an attempt to reduce fare evasion rates on a European public transport system, we first asked paying passengers what word they would use to describe those who dodged their fare. One of most common responses was a "cheater". "Cheater" is an interesting word. It will often elicit anger in people, primarily because there is an immediate source of blame. For some, it will prompt feelings of disassociation and even disgust. Even cheats don't like cheaters.

In our studies we replaced posters alerting fare-dodgers that they risked a fine for not having a ticket, with a much more emotionally charged message describing them as cheats. Fare evasion rates dropped by 16.6% with the effect lasting for almost a year. It appears this was not a fluke. When the approach was replicated on one of Australia's Light Rail systems, fare evasion rates fell by 21.4%, saving millions.[12]

For those charged with influencing and persuading others, provoking emotional responses like anger and disgust could be seen as controversial, even brutal. Yet they can also be effective. Caution is therefore needed to ensure they are used sensitively. It is also worth noting how these two emotive triggers will often be most helpful when addressing challenges that require the influencer to reduce, avoid or stop the incidence of a behaviour. Their use does not necessarily need to be avoided when it comes to activating or increasing specific outcomes, but their close emotional opposites – empathy and awe – might be more productive.

Empathy

The ability to feel and understand the emotions of others – to walk in another's shoes – is at the heart of our humanity. Empathy has the capacity to transcend boundaries, whether naturally occurring ones (like cultures and race) or more manufactured ones such as corporate cultures and department silos. Empathy can be a powerful force for activating, maintaining and repairing relationships and can have a strong bearing on our decision-making. When weighing whether we should follow someone's advice, we might replace the hard question: "Does this person appear to know what they're talking about?" with an easier one: "Does this person appear to care?"

In some instances, empathy can be wholly transformational. Most of us will have personal stories from the covid-19 pandemic where differences were set aside, petty annoyances forgotten (even if only temporarily) and strangers collaborated for the greater good. We wore masks to protect the vulnerable, and set up WhatsApp groups to support neighbours we hardly knew. Although many of these actions were a direct response to imposed rules, the three components of the Influence Equation played a significant role too. Evidence in the form of daily reports of R rates, emerging variants and hospital admissions together with economics such as fines for those who broke the rules had a crucial influence. But arguably it was our emotional responses that had the biggest influence on our actions, many triggered by an abundance of empathy. People started to care a little more. No wonder empathy is often referred to as a community's "social glue". And why it can be such a powerful lever in the influencer's repertoire of tools.

"Be warm and show empathy" is a central message in Dale Carnegie's *How to Win Friends and Influence People*. It is advice that has stood the test of time. Take the work of Nalini

Ambady, a pioneering researcher on snap judgements.[13] She took audiotaped conversations of surgeons speaking to their patients, and played brief extracts to groups of complete strangers. Each extract lasted just ten seconds and immediately afterwards the listeners were asked to rate how empathetic the medics were. On matching these results with the surgeons' professional records, Ambady found something astonishing. Those surgeons rated as more empathetic were six times less likely to have been sued for malpractice.

What they knew was far less significant than whether they cared.

The lesson is not one solely for those working in medicine. All of us who lead and manage people should heed the welcome returns available to those with an empathetic mindset. The uncertainties and complexities inherent in an interconnected, competitive workplace require leaders to be not only competent, but also caring. Genuine empathy has proved to be a well-trodden path to achieving this, despite businesses frequently prioritising competency over empathy. Over time, however, the cost of over-emphasising competence alone can prove costly. Those regarded as leadership masters demonstrate compassion too, affording them the opportunity to forge connections, transcend differences and unite the polarised.

The result? Increased influence.

Awe

Picture a group of boisterous businessmen who, on landing a new deal or profitable trade, leap to their feet, slapping each other's backs and high-fiving in a celebratory, self-aggrandising style. "Awesome," they exclaim loudly. It's an image we can easily construct in our minds. We might view it as flashy or ostentatious – even vulgar. But it's certainly not awesome.

As emotions go, awe is more akin to a cocktail than a shot. An emotive brew of curiosity, amazement and promise, its ability to inspire and persuade is impressive. One reason concerns the diminishing effect that awe can have on personal egos and its igniting effect on the possible. Beau Lotto, a neurologist who has studied awe-inspiring performers including Cirque du Soleil, describes awe as an emotional dish of novelty and dynamism arising from encounters with the extraordinary.[14] Stirring stuff.

Notice, though, that awe is not a solitary pursuit. It has a collective quality which frequently activates a need to connect emotionally with others. Awe explains why people experiencing it unaccompanied often react with an immediate wish for others to join them. There is a lesson here for the weary business traveller. As tempting as it might be to shoehorn an opportunistic visit to the Grand Canyon or Rio's carnival on a business trip, the strong advice is to avoid doing so. Wait to visit with your nearest and I guarantee you will be much happier.

When people think of awe, they usually think of the monumental: inspiring landscapes, extraordinary feats of engineering, the vastness of a night sky or the star-struck wonder of meeting a favourite celebrity. But the expansive quality of awe can be triggered in less grander contexts too. Usefully, awe can be a particularly influential emotion to trigger when the persuasive task faced involves influencing a group to cast aside individual preferences and focus instead on the bigger picture. Such is its power to spotlight a group's needs over their own.

So when drafting a presentation for the next sales meeting or crafting an inspiring conference address, avoid the temptation to open PowerPoint and start copy-and-pasting the latest average quarterly margins or the current state of your sales funnel. At least at first. Much better to consider ways to be a mood maker by first installing a sense of collective awe in your audience. Especially if the goal is to create a sense of group responsibility to business goals.

Awe can even be deployed to promote pro-social behaviours. Paul Piff, a psychologist at the University of California, finds that people experiencing awe are much more likely to agree with statements such as: "I feel I am in the presence of something much greater than myself." They even claim to act more ethically. When Piff enquired about the likelihood of returning money they found to its rightful owner, people experiencing awe showed greater honesty than those experiencing other emotions, such as pride.[15]

It is clear that our emotional state – whether anger, disgust, empathy, awe or myriad other emotions – can have a significant influence on our decisions and subsequent actions. This raises a broader question: how can we increase our influence at work by establishing any of these persuasive emotional states in our audience, readying them for our important message? One approach appears especially effective. It requires us to inject humanity into our appeals through two specific vehicles of emotion.

Vehicles of emotions

Stories, anecdotes and analogies

At the root of almost all successful influence lies an inescapable truth: it's personal. There is a humanity to persuasion. Those able to make even the most basic human connections when delivering their message are more likely to succeed. It is easy to forget this. Modern-day business tools like email and text-based messaging platforms are designed for expediency. Yet their speed and reach coupled with our overuse and dependence comes at a price. Research conducted by Vanessa Bohns, an organisational psychologist at Cornell University and author of *You Have More Influence Than You Think*,[16] finds that face-to-face requests can be as much as 34 times more effective at generating a positive response than the same request sent by email.[17] The recommendation is not necessarily to ditch email, Slack and WhatsApp from your business life. But you should at least avoid falling into the trap of overestimating the effectiveness of these efficient, but ultimately bloodless, forms of communication. If anything, they exert more influence over the user than they do as a useful means for influencing others. A simple – and to some, perhaps horrifying – strategy emerges: pick up the phone and speak to someone.

Even the merest injection of humanity in the data-driven environment in which we now work can make a big difference. When researchers randomly included a passport-sized photograph of a patient on CT scans, medics who saw the face of the person they were diagnosing recommended a greater number of tests and treatments than those who saw scans of patients with a similar prognosis but no photo.[18]

Working with the charity missingpersons.org, my colleague Anita Braga was able to turn poor-resolution mobile phone photos of people who had been reported missing into moving images using AI technology. Displaying these more humanised images on digital advertising screens in addition to changing the words "missing person" to "Help us find (name)" led to increased calls from the public reporting potential sightings.[19]

The use of faces has been shown to be effective in email communications too. When a car-valeting firm included a picture of the person who would be cleaning their vehicle in confirmation emails sent after booking an online appointment, the number of customers who cancelled or were not at home when the company came to clean the car dropped dramatically. It's much easier to ignore a faceless email than one with someone's face attached to it. But why does the humanisation of what are otherwise wholly common messages have such an impact?

Psychologists claim that humanising a message radically alters the way in which information contained in that message is processed. When we are exposed to arguments based on logic and fact it is easier to be naturally dubious and critical about what is being said. But human stories transport us and provide the stage for emotional connections to be made. Interestingly, the humanisation of a message or appeal has been shown to consume audiences to the extent that it often reduces their ability to detect inaccuracies. This is certainly not an invitation to inject humanity as a means of boosting an otherwise weak argument. But assuming we have a good case to make, we would be fools not to exploit their power. The reason is simple: people will argue with your facts and logic, but rarely with your story.

Stories trump statistics. That's why masters of the influence process lead with them. They know that to be ultimately effective they need to involve their audience emotionally before making their proposal. If you want to be influential at work, remember that experiences should always precede explanations, not come after them.

In addition to humanising our persuasive appeals through stories, the use of anecdotes and analogies can create compelling and emotionally connected experiences, preparing audiences to be more receptive to what you say next.

Anecdotes

A short story, observed the Irish novelist William Trevor, "should be an explosion of truth". The same might be said of anecdotes. These succinct, to-the-point narratives that frequently capture attention and sway a crowd tend to be most useful when describing a specific feature or nuance of a topic that illustrates a wider point. A parent explaining to their complaining child that there were only four TV channels in their day, or a manager telling a new recruit that early in their career they plucked up the courage to approach a senior manager which led to a mentorship and future job, are examples of anecdotes.

According to communication scholars, fluency – that is, how easy people find it to process information – is what gives anecdotes their persuasive power. They represent a "narrative fidelity" that resemble an audience's own experiences. And when they do resonate and mirror a reality, many people are willing to accept them as a reliable, engaging and credible source.

Anecdotes are useful for the influential communicator because they act as a bridge that connects information and truth. They add colour to an argument that pallid statistics and abstract data rarely match. Neuroscientists have shown that anecdotes, as well as activating the language-processing parts of our brains, can activate the neurological regions responsible for experiencing emotion through the increased production of oxytocin – the hormone that effects positive attitudes and social bonding.

Literature and history are littered with anecdotes, from *The Great Gatsby* to the *Harry Potter* books. Think Ronald Reagan's: "All great change in America begins at the dinner table" and Bill Clinton's: "Our differences do matter, but our common humanity matters more." But to suggest that anecdotes are limited to the domain of prose and presidents is wrong. Their true persuasive worth is found in the everyday: the admission of a mistake made that connects an audience to a broader lesson learned, a manager publicly acknowledging a team member for their dedication to customer service, a charity appeal highlighting a life transformed. The power of a relatable anecdote to persuade can be very effective, provided that a few basic rules are followed. First, they need to be super-short. Second, they should be conversational. And, most importantly, they should be self-evident. The moment you find yourself explaining your anecdote, it ceases to be one.

Analogies

"It has been well said that an author who expects results from a first novel is in a position similar to that of a man who drops a rose petal down the Grand Canyon of Arizona and listens for the echo."

As analogies go, this one, from P.G. Wodehouse's *Cocktail Time* describing the futility of a first-time author, certainly hits the mark. Harsh? Yes. Vivid and clear with no room for misinterpretation? Also, yes.

Like anecdotes, analogies can serve as effective and persuasive narratives. But they work differently. Anecdotes are stories, usually personal, deployed to initiate an emotional connection. In contrast, analogies are comparisons that make a connection by relating a new concept that a communicator wishes to introduce to something with which their audience will already be familiar.

Analogies leverage a process that cognitive scientists call "structural mapping" – a mechanism that helps us to connect familiar and existing knowledge to novel and less familiar concepts.[20] Think of Einstein's comparison of a person riding on a beam of light with someone running alongside a train to illustrate how time and space are connected. Given their ability to fast-track an audience's understanding of new ideas and concepts, analogies can be helpful when a communicator is attempting to convince their influence target to consider a novel proposition or innovation, particularly an intricate or complex one. Put another way, analogies will often make things easy: a climate scientist comparing our planet's plight with a patient on a critical care ward, a sales rep describing a new product as "like an iPhone, but for dishwashers". Thomas Stemberg, founder of the office supply retailer Staples, pitched to investor communities by claiming that his new stationery chain would be "the Best Buy of office supplies". Even the investors themselves are not immune to using a persuasive analogy or two. When asked how he selects new ventures, Warren Buffett replied that he prioritises his picks by their status as an "economic castle" – surrounded by moats that make it hard for competitors to penetrate.

*

When persuading others, a lesson emerges. Attempting to influence and persuade others by using a dispassionate presentation of evidence and economics alone goes against the grain of our evolved emotional selves. That's not to say that evidence and economics aren't important: they are two of the three nominators in the Influence Equation. But in the same way that a two-legged stool makes for less-than-robust seating, a focus on only evidence and economics makes for a less-than-robust influence strategy. Cold hard facts matter but warmer, softer human sentiment matters too. Why should your boss care about that new initiative you are proposing? How will the innovation you are offering not only save money but also positively affect lives? How will people feel when your new training is implemented?

Whether the influence target is one mind, an entire office or the whole world, it is important to remind ourselves that the route to persuading others is invariably a human one.

PART 3

Influence at work: principles, practices and ethics

Overview

Like many people I enjoy an intriguing concept, interesting idea or fascinating new theory. Especially those that might go some way to explaining the frequently puzzling and sometimes bewildering nature of human behaviour. But, also like many people, I harbour an impatience for an idea that can only prove its worth in theory. In the world of work and business, I find most people are ultimately concerned with results.

My goal in Part 1 and Part 2 of this book was to present a balance of robust and evidence-based information about the persuasion process, coupled with actionable ways that anyone interested in being more influential at work could put into practice. Probably the reason you picked up this book was not just to learn the theory of being more influential at work, but also how to *be* more influential at work. In Part 3, I double down on this endeavour by focusing on the principles, the practice and the ethics of influence.

Start with the principles. A little over 20 years ago I was lucky enough to meet and subsequently study and work with Robert Cialdini, an academic regarded as the world's foremost expert in the psychology of persuasion (and also the most cited). Cialdini has had an outsized influence on my life and career. I will be forever grateful for the opportunity to learn from, work with and publish with the most noted and respected expert in the field.

Cialdini has established his rightful place in social scientific history. When it was first published in 1984 no one could have predicted that his book – *Influence: The Psychology of Persuasion* – would have such an extraordinary impact. With more than 6 million copies sold and continuing to sell in greater numbers than ever, the book has become a staple for business executives, policymakers and world leaders keen to have influence and impact. Like many success stories, the book started humbly. As a newly tenured professor at Arizona State University, Cialdini set out to study and catalogue the tactics and approaches that could be successfully deployed by one person or group to persuade another. He infiltrated numerous "influence settings" like sales training classes, businesses, lobbying groups, even cults. He expected to find thousands of tactics and strategies at work. He found only seven.

Given how foundational Cialdini's work is to the practice of influence, it demands a chapter in its own right. Therefore, Chapter 7 is given over to a summary of the principles of persuasion, including examples of new work on which Cialdini and I have collaborated.

My long association with Bob Cialdini has resulted in me receiving my own fair share of questions from people keen to boost their powers of persuasion. In Chapter 8, I review ten of the more common questions my team and I are asked, and that are based on real-life situations people at work face. Although not guaranteed (no influence approach comes with a cast-iron warranty of effectiveness), I hope the responses to these common influence challenges prove more helpful and insightful than simply guessing or going with your gut.

Finally, in Chapter 9, I turn to the ethics of the influence process. Just because we can influence others doesn't mean we always should, at least not without consideration of the implications and the bigger picture. The chapter is one of the shorter ones in the book, not because the subject is unimportant (it is arguably the most important) but because books like this are written as usable guides and we authors assume good intent. Hence, no morality warnings, admonitions or finger-wagging. Instead, a helpful guide to ensure your new-found influence lands favourably both now and in the longer term without any need to compromise your values or integrity.

7

The principles of influence

This chapter reviews Robert Cialdini's seven universal principles of influence, which are based on his years of scientific research and are comprehensively presented in his seminal book *Influence: The Psychology of Persuasion*.[1] Consider the principles as a set of tools which, when used appropriately and in the right context, can trigger agreement in others.

Like any set of tools, some work best in specific instances and circumstances. Although it's possible to make a hole in a wall using a screwdriver and a hammer, it's usually far more efficient to use a drill. The analogy holds true for the principles of influence. Some principles address specific influence challenges and are suited to certain contexts. I will review them in the order that most find helpful and that also answers a question I am frequently asked: which principle of persuasion will be most useful in a specific situation?

The answer comes from an insight identified and developed by another colleague, Dr Gregory Niedert. Niedert astutely observes that while all of us face a near-limitless range of influence challenges, at work and in our personal lives, the vast majority can be neatly categorised in one of three ways. In other words, there are only three overarching influence challenges that people face.

The first are *relationship-based* challenges. To persuade

an individual or a group, you will probably need to build a connection with them. Until that connection is established, your influence is likely to stall. Examples might include reaching out to prospective new clients, gaining access to decision-makers, growing your network of contacts, or maybe repairing an existing relationship that has faltered. Three of Cialdini's seven influence principles are particularly useful in relationship-based influence challenges: the principles of reciprocity, liking and unity.

The second category is *decision-based* challenges, which concern reducing people's uncertainty about an idea or proposition you want them to consider. You may have an existing connection and relationship with the people you want to persuade, but they might harbour doubts about your proposal. Doubts and uncertainty can kill a persuasive appeal. The challenge is how to reduce people's uncertainty in a way that increases credibility and trust in your idea, allowing them to decide. Two other Cialdini principles can help: the principles of authority and social proof.

The third influence category, *action-based* challenges, relate to persuading people to actually do something. Even with an established relationship and an audience reassured and convinced about your idea or proposition, there is often a gap between the intention to do something and actually doing it. To address action-based challenges, Cialdini's two remaining principles are most likely to be useful: the principles of consistency and scarcity.

Relationship-based influence challenges

Principle 1. Reciprocity

People give back to others the gift or service that they first received

After observing their children scoff Happy Meals and play boisterously in the ball pit with the other kids, parents who make a weekend trip to one of McDonald's fast-food restaurants in Bogota, Colombia know that one final moment of joy awaits. As they coax their exhausted offspring back to the car, staff are on hand to distribute large, red balloons – one per child. A reminder of a fun time had by all.

Let's be clear about what's happening here. The balloons aren't just souvenirs. They are good for business too. Happy kids mean happy parents. And happy parents return, boosting sales.

The success of this simple strategy goes some way to explaining the reluctance of restaurant managers to follow a suggestion made by the psychologist Helen Mankin and me to make a subtle change to their balloon policy. Their hesitation was understandable: why tinker with a winning formula? But Mankin and I believed we were on to something and so we persevered. Eventually the managers agreed to put their initial scepticism to one side and try an experiment. Immediately after the tests began, stores measured a 20% increase in sales ... of coffee.[2]

The change we suggested was simple. Instead of giving children a balloon when they leave the restaurant, give them one when they arrive. But why would this subtle and costless change make such a difference? Because most people feel an obligation to give back to others the form of service, gift or favour they have first received. A balloon given to children as they leave the restaurant serves as a reward for visiting. But a balloon given at the entrance ceases to be a reward and instead becomes a gift. And as the societal rule mandates, if you give something to me, then I should give something back. In the case of McDonald's, the reciprocity came in the form of increased orders.

But why coffee – an item that children are unlikely to order? There's a straightforward reason of which all parents are aware. A gift given to a child is really a gift given to their parents. It's easy to see how a parent might return the favour by buying themselves a cup of coffee.

The McDonalds experiment is a simple illustration of the first of Cialdini's principle of influence: *reciprocity*. People say yes to those who they owe. Not every time. We all know someone happy to accept the assistance, goodwill or help of another, without experiencing any emotional burden or sense of duty to respond in kind. The couple in the flat upstairs who happily let their neighbours put out their recycling when they are on holiday but never return the favour. The colleague whose turn to make (or buy) the coffee always seems to coincide with an "urgent" client call. We have names for these people: cadgers, scroungers, freeloaders.

However, notice something. We may regard them as freeloaders, but their unwillingness to reciprocate is not costless to them. They pay a social price. They might be socially chastised. Pens might strike their names from invitation lists. Serial offenders might be scorned entirely. In the context of the fundamental human motivations of accuracy, connection and ego, reciprocity creates and maintains connections between others. Those who conduct themselves appropriately within the orbit of social obligation benefit by way of greater connection. They bond and gain the approval of others. They are more likely to have larger networks. They engage with people on a deeper level. In short, they possess a more favourable context for influence.

Reciprocity is fundamental to cooperation between people and plays an important role in the effectiveness of teams too. Those who proactively seek to help and support others by exchanging resources typically prosper more, not only at work but also in communities and societies. No surprise, then, why parents teach their children from their earliest years not to take without giving in return. But perhaps they are merely reinforcing what's already there. Evolutionary research has shown that children are likely to respond to the rule of "give and take" before they reach the age of two. No wonder reciprocity is such a potent tool for those seeking to grow their influence.

Giving first

Imagine, after checking into a hotel room, you notice a card in the bathroom asking you to reuse your towels as part of the hotel's conservation programme. Further, you learn that some guests (yourself included) have been offered an incentive to boost the programme's effectiveness. If you reuse your towels a donation will be made to a local conservation charity. Does this added incentive increase compliance to reusing your towels? Many would expect the addition of this benevolent act to improve recycling rates. But in a series of studies, my long-term colleague Noah Goldstein – a social psychologist at the Anderson Business School, UCLA – found the opposite. Guests offered this charitable "carrot" were much less likely to reuse their towels.[3]

The results appear puzzling. Perhaps guests don't trust the hotel, a profit-making concern, to donate. Or maybe the charity selected wasn't popular with the guests. Both reasons might account for the scheme's failure. But there is another explanation, which lies within the principle of reciprocity. Notice that guests are only rewarded when they reuse their towels. Essentially the hotel is saying: "If you do this for us, only then we will do this for you." In this context, guests have to act first, not the hotel. The rule mandates a "give and take" approach. But the hotel is operating a "take and give" approach, which is not how the rule of reciprocity works.

Savvy marketeers know this. A free sample or trial can lead to a significant uplift in sales that more than compensates firms for any initial "cost" they incur. Contributors to political campaigns often find themselves benefactors of friendly policies, lobbying power and access. And guests who were informed their hotel had *already* donated to an environmental charity on their behalf were, in Goldstein's studies, 47% more likely to reuse their towels.[4] There is a clear implication. If you want to encourage people to do something for you, do something for them first.

What should you give?

In the 20-odd years I have been researching, writing about and applying the science and practice of influence, I have noticed a subtle shift in what appears to motivate people to give back to others what they have first been granted, especially at work and in business. In my early career days tangible gifts and goodies were the mainstay of mutual backscratching: tickets to a sporting event, sponsorship to attend a conference, free lunches, corporate knick-knacks like pens, polo shirts and umbrellas with the name and logo of the donor organisation prominently displayed. Although some of these perks remain commonplace, two forces appear to have reduced their impact. The first is regulation. Many firms now have policies forbidding employees from accepting inducements for fear they unduly orient attention not to the optimal vendor but rather to the obligating one. The sweetener, it seems, is not as sweet as it once was.

A second reason concerns what I am increasingly witnessing as an abundance of offers. Many are subject to increasing numbers of companies and their representatives offering free subscriptions, samples and all manner of trinkets designed to induce obligations which, let's be in no doubt, are designed as a starting point for influence. This is unlikely to diminish any time soon. Firms identify and provide gifts to "influencers" on social media in the knowledge that a highly visible tweet or Instagram post of their wares can frequently result in "sold out" stocks, driving sales further. But not everyone can be an influencer, and not everyone has the unlimited budget needed to be a profligate giver. What can we ordinary folks do to boost our persuasive prowess that doesn't require the distribution of expensive giveaways or millions of online followers?

One answer is to recognise the limits of tangible, material gifts and instead focus on providing more intangible ones. The giving of tangible gifts comes with a good chance that someone else will come along and offer something bigger or better than we can afford, crowding out our own well-meaning but, as it turns out, inadequate attempts. Giving becomes a turf war where the winner is the one who offers the most. The result is people become accustomed to receiving more and more. Expectations are raised and the personal nature of reciprocation is diminished.

This is less the case with intangible gifts, precisely because of their inherently personal nature. By intangible gifts, I mean anything you cannot buy in a shop or online: human things like your time, a sympathetic ear, a genuine compliment, an expression of empathy, a well-timed piece of advice, a referral, or your trust.

If you want people to trust you, show that you trust them first. If you want people to listen to you, listen to them first. And if you want people to help you, help them first.

Not just what, but how

How you provide help and give to others matters too. In one study waiters and waitresses who offered customers a single mint alongside their bill received tips that were on average 3% higher than tips from customers who were not given a mint. For customers given two mints, average tips increased by 14%, demonstrating an important insight for would-be persuaders. People often prioritise significance over costliness. Two mints are more significant than one, but mints are hardly expensive. The study offers a useful reminder: costly gifts may well be significant, but significant gifts need not be costly.

Perhaps the most telling insight from these studies comes from a third condition. Waiters and waitresses placed the bill on the table along with a single mint. After retreating, they appeared a moment later and placed a second mint on the table. Still two mints but now delivered in an unexpected way. The result? An increase of more than 20% in tips.[5]

There is a clear implication for anyone wishing to persuade others through the principle of reciprocity. Not only should you consider carefully *what* you give, potentially prioritising the intangible over the tangible, but you should also pay careful attention to *how* you give. Giving in significant and unexpected ways can elevate the worth of the same gift in the receiver's eye, resulting in an increased chance of them wanting to give back. But there is one other factor that seems to have the biggest impact of all: personalisation.

Imagine you have just returned from a business trip or holiday and, as you push open your front door, you meet with resistance from the pile of letters, mailings and circulars delivered while you've been away. As you scoop them up, you have a decision to make. Which do you attend to first? It's the letter with your name and address handwritten on the envelope. Why? Because it has been personalised.

Personalisation propels persuasion. In an increasingly transactional world, even relatively low levels of personalisation can make a difference. Randy Garner, a Texas-based psychologist, found he could double the number of people who completed his surveys if he attached a handwritten message on a Post-it note to his questionnaires.[6] It worked for the same reason you open the letter from the person who took the trouble to handwrite your name and address on the envelope. Unlike most communications that compete for attention (and, in the case of bills, your cash), a handwritten message stands out because someone has taken the trouble to personalise it.

Handwritten notes are not the only way to personalise persuasive appeals. In his book *Pre-Suasion*,[7] Robert Cialdini cites the story of Abu Jandal, a former bodyguard of Osama bin Laden, who was captured and questioned in a Yemeni prison shortly after the terror attacks on September 9th 2001. Early attempts to elicit valuable intelligence proved futile until interrogators noticed that, despite eating most of the food he was served, he never touched the biscuits that were often placed on his food tray. Jandal was a diabetic. Learning this, and subsequently providing sugar-free biscuits was, according to one intelligence officer, an important key in turning him.

No one knows whether this act alone was causal in changing the dynamic. But it is not too much of a stretch to suggest this act of personalisation could have played an important part. This is the power of reciprocity as a tool of influence. Notice, how this example demonstrates the reach of reciprocity. The principle creates connections not just within our own tribes and cultures, but across others too.

What flows from reciprocity? Appreciation, exchange and influence

Our social obligations to others are frequently the result of us accepting their initial help and assistance. It is the act of providing help and resources to others *first* that installs a sense of obligation, particularly when what was given or offered is deemed unexpected, significant and personalised. And in that context of social obligation, people are more inclined to express their appreciation to us, which raises an important consideration. What do you say to someone who thanks you for something you did for them first?

One thing the savvy persuader will never say is: "Well I've helped you, so now you owe me!" They know that doing so will ensure that person never comes to them again. But they are also unlikely to say: "No problem", "I was happy to help" or "Think nothing of it." This is because they recognise the persuasive power that exists immediately after earning a thank you. Because people are generally predisposed to say yes to those they have just thanked, perhaps this is a good moment for a business development executive to seek an appointment. Or for the financial adviser to request a referral, or for Sam and Jake to ask for the resources they need to deliver on next quarters projects, or to ask whether those distracted parents in Colombian burger restaurants fancy buying a cup of coffee while they watch their children playing.

Reciprocity at work
- Don't ask: "Who can help me?" Instead ask: "Who can I help?"

- If the request you have is important, ditch the email and take the personal approach instead. Send a handwritten note or pick up the phone.

- What do you usually say after you receive a genuine thank you? What could you say instead to win a favour back or pay a favour forward?

Principle 2. Liking

People prefer to say yes to those they know and like

People prefer to say yes to the people they like. Although many things might trigger one person to like another, two stand out: commonalities and compliments.

We've all experienced a sense of affinity to someone soon after meeting them. Sitting at the heart of this near-instant connection will frequently be something shared: we went to the same school, we drive the same make of car, have children of the same age, a friend in common, or similar sounding names.

When a group of psychologists sent out requests to random strangers asking if they would complete a survey, one group was significantly more inclined to complete and return it. Unlike the surveys that Randy Garner sent with a personalised Post-it note stuck on the front, these requests contained a different but equally potent signal of connection. The requester had a similar name to the recipient. A person called Robert Greer might receive a survey sent from someone named Bob Gregar. A woman named Cynthia Johnston might get a survey from someone called Cindy Johanson. Those receiving the survey from someone with a similar name were almost twice as likely to complete and return it. Yet none of the participants, when asked later, identified that it was the similarity of the sender's name that persuaded them to complete the form.[8]

Like the principle of reciprocity, the principle of liking is a connector of people. As a result, it is generally most helpful in situations where there's a need to build a relationship or a network with people before persuading them. Take negotiations. In one experiment, executives were tasked with negotiating on a large deal. Half were reminded that "time is money" and that they should get down to business quickly. The other half were encouraged to spend a few moments getting to know a bit about each other in an attempt to find commonalities and make a connection. This social investment proved worthwhile. Compared with the nearly 30% who deadlocked in the "straight down to business group", only 6% of those who sought out commonalities before haggling were unable to agree a deal. Intriguingly, when outcomes of all the negotiations were measured, those who sought commonalities with each other walked away with a much better deal for both parties – as much as an 18% increase. Seeking similarities with co-workers, colleagues and potential clients before deal making seems to increase not only the chances of an agreement but also the chances of receiving a larger slice of the pie you agreed.[9]

Most fascinating was that these experiments were all conducted online. Post-pandemic, the widespread adoption of hybrid working means that many of our influence challenges are now carried out virtually. This study provides a useful reminder that behind that screen of pixels is a human who is subject to exactly the same fundamental motivations to connect with others as we are. When it comes to influence, ignoring or disregarding this in exchange for haste and efficiency is a fool's errand.

Compliments

Most people like receiving compliments. Most people also give little thought to their openness to being influenced immediately after being given a compliment. One study found that people are more likely to respond favourably to a request from a colleague if they receive a compliment from that co-worker immediately before the request is made.[10] Interestingly, people agreed to help regardless of how likeable the requester was, which suggests that compliments often work without the need for any existing congeniality.

This is not an isolated example. Numerous studies have demonstrated the benefits of buttering up. Waiters receive larger tips after complimenting customers on their menu selection. Hair stylists get bigger tips after telling clients how much they like their new hairdo, despite the compliment-giver being complicit in the coiffe. Other research shows that people are susceptible to compliments even when they are aware the flatterer has an ulterior motive.[11]

Compliments activate liking because they provide emotional validation. "I can live for two months on a good compliment," said Mark Twain, who rightly identified that expressions of gratitude and praise boost people's sense of well-being and self-esteem. They are a gift, of sorts. And we all know what the rule for gift giving says we must do in response.

This is not to advocate that, in pursuit of a quick persuasive win, you should resort to sycophancy or disingenuous toadyism. For an important reason. False flattery, even if it is potentially effective, creates a barrier to something far more meaningful and authentic: to find something genuinely complimentary about another person. Counter-intuitively, it can be particularly effective to find something likeable about people you may actively dislike but still have to work with.

This "charm and disarm" can work for two reasons. First, it creates a connection. And connection is the starting point for influence. Realise too that you don't have to limit yourself to complimenting others in only personal ways, which is helpful for those you find objectionable. The strategy also works when complimenting them on work-related features you like or admire: their dedication to work or the fact they always deliver on their promises.

The second reason why focusing on an admirable feature held by someone you find difficult to deal with is that you might start to notice other likeable aspects about them. This is important because, although the principle of liking suggests that people are more likely to be persuaded by those who they like, there is one person people are even more likely to be persuaded by. The person who likes them, and says as much.

This insight calls into question a rule to which many sales professionals will attest: the first rule of sales is to get your customer to like you. Although I see no downsides to a customer liking a salesperson, I would argue there is something even more compelling about a salesperson liking their customers. A moment of quick reflection shows why. The person who genuinely likes you probably has your best interests at heart. In that context you can draw breath, relax a little and lower your guard. And the door to influence opens a little wider.

Liking at work

- Liking flows from commonalities and compliments, where a road to yes lies ahead.
- We say yes to people we like, but we are even more likely to say yes to the people who we know like us.

- Discovering shared commonalities and giving genuine compliments is a potent route to influence, even with those we may not currently like.

Principle 3. Unity

People say yes to those they see as one of their own

The coronavirus pandemic shone a spotlight on much that is good about the human condition, and a considerable amount of what is bad. On the plus side, many communities became more closely connected, at least temporarily. People chatted with their neighbours more and offered a helping hand to the defenceless and vulnerable. Essential workers like doctors and nurses were applauded. People even joined WhatsApp groups to share information about good walks discovered, top tips for making sourdough, and updates on which supermarkets had supplies of toilet roll.

On the downside, there was polarisation. Many lamented the policies adopted by their governments. Others breached the rules (or interpreted them in flexible, self-serving ways), including the lawmakers who set them. Some people were sceptical of vaccines, highlighting that, given their speedy production, no one could be sure of their long-term effects. Others had more extreme views: there was no virus, the pandemic was a context for the establishment of a new world order. And certainly, you should avoid the vaccines; they weren't designed to protect, but to control.

Regardless of the positives and negatives, the pandemic illustrated an important factor at the heart of what influences actions and perspectives: your identity. Who you are exerts a powerful sway on who you chose to unite with and who you don't. The implications for influence are considerable.

The successful persuader intuitively seems to recognise the

power of social identities and the strong feeling of unity that arises from them. They know that when it comes to influencing others, it is not always the evidence or the economics of a case being made that counts but how the case being made emanates from one of their own. This is the principle of unity.

The principle of unity is not about simple similarities. That's the principle of liking. Unity is about the categories and labels people use to define themselves and seek kinship with others, like race, ethnicity, nationality, political and religious affiliations and, of course, family. When you hear a request or proposition from someone in your group, unity doesn't influence your inclination to say yes just because you like them (or they like you). Unity tips the balance of their appeal because you *are one of them*.

When social psychologist Mark Levine, at the University of Lancaster, arranged for football fans to encounter someone who needed help (an injured runner) moments after discussing the love for their team, they were much more likely to offer help if the unfortunate jogger's shirt was the same colour as their team's. And they were much less likely to help when the shirt colour was different.[12] Research demonstrates that this effect doesn't hold just for football supporters. People are more likely to take the advice of a financial adviser who shares the same political affiliations as their own more than the advice of an adviser who does not. Studies in the United States reveal that people are also more inclined to vaccinate their children if the political party they voted for is currently in office.

Surely, though, when facing a decision or judgement, people are more inclined to be persuaded by the messenger who is sharing a concrete insight rather than one who merely shares a common identity. They might, but not always. Take, for example, an intriguing series of studies conducted by two of my colleagues, psychologists Joseph Marks and Eloise Copland.[13]

In the studies, people exchanged information about each other (including personal and political views) before playing a simple shape categorisation game where they could win money. As the game progressed it became clear that two players were particularly good. (The two experts were stooges.) To do equally well and win more cash, the other players merely had to copy these experts. The rub, of course, was that the personal views and opinions of these better performers were dissimilar to their own. What do the other players do? The logical thing would be to set aside polarised views and pocket the money. In reality, though, two-thirds of the players ignored the experts, choosing instead to go with their own intuition. An intuition that was no more certain than a coin toss. That may sound absurd, but it's also human.

The studies by Marks and Copland offer an unsettling but nonetheless important insight for anyone seeking to increase their influence at work. When it comes to the factors that people prioritise in their decision-making, intelligence can come a distant second to identity.

Professional identities, and place

When presenting an idea, putting forward a proposal or seeking to get agreement on a proposition, the advice is to highlight the existence of any genuine unity that exits between the presenter and their audience before delivering an appeal. Two kinds of unity seem especially important: professional identities and place.

Emphasising the existence of a genuine, shared professional history is sensible. Rather than launching straight into an appeal, take time to direct an influence target's attention to the existence of any unquestionable unity. "We've been working in this company together for 20 years and have its best interests at heart." Location matters too. This is because people have developed tendencies to look more favourably on those who, outside work and home, live near them. It's why people are more likely to pay their taxes when told that those who live in the same town have already paid; why citizens are more likely to register to vote when the request comes from a member of their own community (rather than from an official letter or politician); and complete a survey after finding out that the person asking attended the same university as them.

Contact and synchronicity

But what of situations where there is little existing unity? Workplaces, after all, are a melting point of diversity and difference. How do you build unity in these circumstances? Two main things seem to matter: frequency of contact, and the synchronising activities.

Regular contact boosts exposure which, in turn, can increase trust, which elevates your influence. To persuade others, be in the regular presence of those others. Synchronicity matters too. There's a reason why armies march, even though they rarely walk to battlegrounds. The harmonisation of their steps, to the same beat and cadence, creates a united group. Like an orchestra. The skilled persuader seeks to do the same by co-developing projects and proposals rather than producing them in isolation. For example, rather than asking for an influence target's feedback or opinions on a particular project or programme, ask instead for their advice on it. When we ask for feedback we will often receive criticism. But, as the American literary genius Saul Bellow observed, when we ask for advice we are more likely to get an accomplice. And that's a good thing because accomplices are more likely to view themselves as united with us.

Unity at work

- Highlight the existence of identity-relevant similarities before attempting to influence others.
- To create a sense of unity, seek out opportunities to co-develop proposals and ideas rather than working alone.
- Ask for advice rather than feedback.

Decision-based influence challenges

Principle 4. Authority

People look to experts to guide the way

One sunny weekend in 1968 psychologists Anthony Doob and Alan Gross drove around Palo Alto in northern California seeking answers to a question they had been pondering. What percentage of drivers toot their horn when the car in front is holding up traffic? Their research concluded that Californian drivers were an impatient lot. On average seven out of ten hit their horn when held up by the car ahead. But their frustration was uneven. Motorists were much more likely to honk at cheaper, beat-up cars, and considerably less at sleeker, more expensive models. It would appear that a driver's likelihood to honk the horn is influenced by the relative status of the car that's delaying them.[14]

It's not only cars that can evoke such reactions. A similar effect holds true for clothes. Three times as many people contravened a "Don't cross" pedestrian traffic light and followed a man walking across a road when he was wearing a business suit and carrying a briefcase, than when he was wearing jeans and a T-shirt.[15] In another study, patients at a healthcare centre remembered more of what the nurse said to them if the nurse wore a stethoscope while giving advice.[16]

Studies like these show the powerful influence of what psychologists call "trappings of authority". Trappings of authority are visible cues that result in those who possess them being afforded increased attention. But there is a distinction between signs conveying whether someone is *in* authority and signs that someone is *an* authority. Sleek cars and smart suits might signal someone's positional authority, but they are unreliable signs of credibility and expertise. And it is these last two attributes that are far more important when growing one's influence at work. Those who are influenced by your position may be complying only because you have the power to reward or punish them. But those who see you as a legitimate expert are persuaded, not via hierarchy or control but because you have a standing worth following. For example, in a series of studies conducted by Bob Cialdini, physiotherapists who displayed their diplomas on treatment room walls increased the number of patients who complied with their home exercise regimes by more than 30%. Cars and clothes might indicate that you are "in" authority. But certificates and credentials tend to be more effective at signalling you are "an" authority.[17]

Authority's moments

People typically seek out the wisdom and expertise of others when they face an uncertain situation or feel anxious about what they should do next. This makes sense. None of us can be knowledgeable about everything. Far more efficient, and certainly less taxing, is to defer to those with a particular talent or specialist knowledge when navigating a complex world. It is during these uncertain moments that an acknowledged authority demonstrates their instrumental value. And it's also why society benefits from some people being plumbers and mechanics, and others being doctors and accountants. But which features of an authority are likely to increase the chances that it is you who is sought out for advice and insight rather than someone else? Two factors seem especially important: credibility and trust.

Credible authorities

Recall the study my colleagues and I conducted with a group of London-based estate agents, described in Chapter 4. They were able to increase the number of appointments booked and secure more signed contracts because their experience and credentials were introduced to prospective clients before they delivered their pitch. Clearly, introductions matter, and so make sure your credibility and expertise are introduced properly before you present or deliver a proposition. This goes for written proposals too. It is a mistake to relegate team biographies to the last pages of pitch and tender documents. They should appear near the front, for the straightforward reason that credibility needs to be established before the message is delivered, not after it.

But what about situations where you need to introduce your expertise but don't have someone to speak on your behalf, as for one-to-one appointments? Here the recommendation is to arrange for your expertise to be introduced in advance via an introductory email or text message. This is easily done by sending your welcome note and agenda with a two-line biography that summarises your expertise and experience. Online meetings provide an opportunity too. On virtual calls, be sure to include your official title or qualifications in the graphic at the bottom of the screen that contains your name. One firm of financial professionals reported an increase in follow-up appointments and referrals when they legitimately included their qualifications (e.g. CFP, APFS) alongside their name. This makes sense. Investing your money with Robert Cranston, FPC is likely to be more reassuring than plain old Bob.

Trusted authorities

But even the most qualified and experienced communicators will struggle to be persuasive if they are not deemed to be trustworthy. As we have already highlighted, trust is something developed over time and through multiple, consistent interactions. But what happens in situations where you don't have years or months to build trust? What if you only have minutes?

Although hard, it is not impossible. There are two routes. The first is to ensure that any proposition or proposal offered is presented in an honest and impartial fashion by deploying the two-sided argument described in Chapter 4. The second is to ensure that any two-sided appeal is presented in a specific order, with the downside always presented before the upsides.

This might seem counter-intuitive, but a closer look reveals the inherent wisdom in such a strategy. All proposals and propositions have both strengths and drawbacks, yet many communicators fall into the trap of describing the most attractive and appealing features of their ideas first, choosing to reserve the declaration of any weakness or drawbacks in their case until the end of their presentation – or never. But the communicator who alerts their audience to a weakness in their case early on is often regarded as more trustworthy. And it is in the context of this newly established perceived trustworthiness that the upsides in their case can land more favourably with their audience, who are now better primed to receive them.

This linguistic jujitsu explains why lawyers often highlight a weakness in a case on their own terms before an opponent has the opportunity to do so; how politicians who compliment an opponent will often be rated as more reasonable by members of both parties; and why advertising messages that direct attention to a downside often experience a boost in sales. Listerine, a mouthwash never applauded for its taste, successfully campaigned on the slogan: "The taste you hate, twice a day."

Perhaps the most important feature of this weakness-first-then-strengths strategy, is how to transition between them. Favourites are the words "but" and its fancier cousin "however". Anyone who has received initial praise from a superior for a job well done and then heard them utter the word "but" will be wholly aware of its rug-pulling capabilities. "Take everything you heard before I was mentioned," says this seemingly harmless little word, "and disregard it. Concentrate, instead, on what comes after me."

Another factor the consummate influencer needs to consider is which weakness to highlight first. Certainly any drawbacks should be small ones. The 17th-century French moralist François de La Rochefoucauld said: "We only confess our little faults to persuade people that we have no big ones."[18] The advice for any proposition that has a large problem or issue is to fix the problem rather than persuade people about a dud. But where there's an opportunity to highlight a small drawback or weakness, research suggests that "'two-sided" persuasive appeals are most effective when there is a clear connection between the negative and positive attributes being communicated. This means that if your goal is primarily to increase the perception of your own trustworthiness, the weaknesses you convey probably matter less. But if you want to increase the trustworthiness of your proposal, you should ensure any dark cloud you confess to is immediately followed by a convincing silver lining.

Authority at work

- Whenever and wherever possible, establish your credibility and expertise before presenting your idea or proposal.
- Build trustworthiness by using two-sided arguments highlighting the weaknesses and drawbacks in your case first.
- Remember the "but" when transitioning to the strengths of your proposal.

Principle 5. Social proof

People follow multiple, comparable others

With three scoops of Madagascan vanilla bean ice cream, chunks of Chuao chocolate, Parisian candied fruits, truffles and marzipan cherries, all topped with a generous drizzle of Armagnac and edible gold leaf, diners ordering the Golden Opulence Sundae at the Serendipity 3 restaurant on New York's upper-east side should arrive with a healthy appetite. And a bulging wallet. Priced at $1,000, it is easily one of the world's most expensive desserts.

Ridiculously lavish sweets invariably attract attention, leading to a steady stream of orders from well-heeled, showboating clients. Not so, however, for the owners of humbler eating establishments who might struggle to persuade customers to order a crème brûlée or apple pie at the end of their meal. Help is at hand, though, in the form of a simple persuasive appeal that reliably increases the sale of desserts without the need for any conspicuous vulgarity or an eye-watering price tag. Alongside the most popular dessert, restaurant owners are advised to place a message truthfully stating that it is "our most popular dessert".

Numerous studies have demonstrated how this honest alert can increase sales of desserts, typically by up to 18%. In one study, conducted in McDonald's restaurants in South America, the effect was considerably larger. Pointing out the most commonly ordered dessert on menu boards led to a 55% increase in sales of McFlurrys.[19] There's a simple reason why: the principle of social proof. The powerful tool of persuasion that states how people often choose what is right for them by looking at the behaviours of comparable others.

Social proof messages are not limited to the promotion of desserts. A similar approach can be used to encourage the consumption of much healthier snacks, like fruit and veg. In one study, Dutch schoolchildren increased their intake of fruit by 35% after being told their fellow classmates enjoyed fruit. In an unsurprising act of juvenile defiance, they also rejected the notion that their peers had had any impact on their new-found love of apples and oranges.[20]

Anything you can do

There are many reasons why the behaviour of others has such a powerful pull on our own. Accuracy, one of the three fundamental motivations outlined in Chapter 2, is an important one. The fact others are doing something sends a strong signal that it is not just the thing that people do, but potentially also the right thing to do in such circumstances. When hundreds of people run from a building shouting "Fire!", following them seems like the right thing to do. Similarly, a long queue outside a restaurant signals that it could be a good place to eat. A second fundamental motivation – connection – also plays a role. By following the crowd, we become the crowd. And with that new allegiance comes other potential advantages like new social connections and, in some cases, even increased protection.

Besides providing a helpful cue of accuracy and the potential for connection, social proof information offers up another useful signal: feasibility. The fact many similar people are doing something might suggest we are able to as well. If most of my colleagues complete their timesheets and expenses on time, then I should be able to. And if my closest neighbours use less energy in their homes, then our family should be able to reduce our consumption too. This last example is not mere conjecture. Energy consumption has been a popular target for testing social proof messages for well over a decade, demonstrating how households will frequently reduce their energy consumption after learning that their comparable neighbours already have.[21] Not only are these programmes broadly effective, but they also come with the advantage of being much cheaper to implement than many other energy-reduction measures. There is a clear reason why. After learning what many others are doing, any lingering doubts about the feasibility of replicating a similar action are, rather like their energy bills, now reduced.

Everybody's doing it
Pointing to the popularity of something has, itself, become popular. As a consequence, appeals based on the principle of social proof have become a mainstay of the communicator's playbook for governments and commercial organisations alike. People are more likely to pay their taxes when told others like them have paid theirs; more likely to choose the "most popular" broadband package when selecting from a list of options; and

more likely to buy a cup of coffee on an aircraft if they see two or more passengers sitting near them buy a drink.[22]

At first glance, it would appear that social proof messages are so powerful they should be a mainstay of any persuasive attempt. But I urge caution. Social proof is not a cure-all. In fact, there are certain contexts and environments where using a social proof message is likely to register a reduced impact or be entirely ineffective.

One is when a preference already exists. Despite our misgivings, a number of managers in South American McDonalds restaurants, buoyed by the impact of the social proof message on dessert sales, thought they should try placing a similar message of popularity on their menu of burgers. A few weeks later we received an email conveying their disappointment at finding no effect and validating our hesitation. Why didn't the message of social proof work? Because customers had little use for information about what others had ordered, as most of them already knew what burger they would choose.[23] People are most inclined to look to others' actions as a guide in situations where they are uncertain. Like the principle of authority, the principle of social proof is most useful when persuading others who face uncertainty or are deciding on something discretionary. Like a dessert.

Another context where social proof messages may not be as effective is when they are delivered electronically, rather than in a physical form or in person. One study designed to recruit people to take part in a market research initiative offered, via email, the chance for participants to win £250. The emails also used a range of persuasive appeals including an altruism message ("please help others"), a loss-aversion message ("don't lose this opportunity") and a social proof message ("many others have participated"). Only the loss-aversion message registered any effect. In another online study designed to persuade people to register as an organ donor, a message of social proof ("thousands of people who visit this website decide to register") was trumped by a message that simply pointed out that "three people die every day because there are not enough organ donors".[24]

I am not suggesting that messages of social proof will invariably be less effective in online contexts. However, and here I am speculating, it is possible messages that leverage a human-centred appeal like social proof might have increased influence when delivered via a human-channel such as a letter or in person, rather than through an electronic channel like an emotionless email.

Regardless, there is one context where I am confident that the use of a social proof message is likely to backfire entirely: when raising awareness of an unwanted or undesirable action that needs to be addressed. Imagine, for example, you are a manager frustrated at the increasing number of meetings that start late. Tardy colleagues rob everyone of the most scarce of commodities, their time. As well as being impolite, delayed starts can lead to inefficiencies like rushed decision-making and have knock-on effects for the next meeting which also starts late. It is reasonable, then, for a frustrated manager to lament: "People seem to have so little regard for others' time that many meetings never start on time." One can sympathise with the manager's approach. Highlighting the regrettable frequency of late-starting meetings should make people realise their negative impact and, as a consequence, change their behaviour. Yet the opposite is more likely to occur, with late-starting meetings becoming even more common. Why? Because lurking within the manager's message lies a much more damaging and potentially normalising one: "Meetings *never* start on time."

Shining a light on the frequent occurrence of unwelcome behaviour isn't limited to office gatherings. Pointing out the large number of colleagues who fail to submit their timesheets promptly, who have yet to complete the annual cultural survey or who park in a space reserved for visitors, often results in an increase, not a decrease, in those behaviours.

A similar phenomenon occurs outside the workplace. Highlighting the number of people who text while driving, fail to pay their taxes, drop litter or shoplift is an unhelpful use of social proof and will potentially backfire. "Look at all these people who do this undesirable thing," is the message delivered. The case of litter is particularly illustrative. Notice litter typically congregates in places that are already littered.

The advice is to avoid using any social proof message that risks popularising the very action you are hoping to curtail. Instead, spotlight attention on the legitimate frequency of desirable actions. In the UK, the National Health Service (NHS) has a perennial problem. Many people fail to turn up to their medical appointments, or cancel in advance, resulting in costly losses for all concerned. In attempt to address the issue some healthcare managers highlighted the problem by publishing the number of patients who missed their appointment the previous month. Our research found these messages promoted rather than reduced no-shows. Learning that many people fail to show makes it potentially easier for others to do so too. "No big deal: everyone else is doing it." There was a second reason. By highlighting the number of patients who missed their appointment via signs on waiting room walls, the only patients who saw them were those doing the right thing and turning up. Not only was the message wrong, but it was also delivered to the wrong audience. After changing the signs in NHS health centres to highlight that most patients arrive on time (or asking people to call 24 hours in advance if they need to cancel), no-shows dropped considerably.[25]

Social proof at work

- Don't rely on your own powers of persuasion to influence people. Use signals of popularity and testimonials to highlight what others are genuinely doing.

- Make sure the examples of social proof you use match the circumstances of those you seek to persuade. If you are persuading a small business owner, use the social proof of other small business owners.

- Avoid the backfiring effect by pointing to desirable actions, not unwanted ones.

Action-based influence challenges

Principle 6. Commitment and consistency

People encounter personal and interpersonal pressure to behave consistently with their commitments

Like many children in the 1980s, I enjoyed entering competitions run by the manufacturers of breakfast cereal. Although the prizes differed – a BMX bike, camping equipment, a year's subscription to *Smash Hits* – the competition structure was always the same.

First was the task itself. Children might be asked to draw a picture, write a story, or answer a few simple questions. Or, in one example, take a photo consuming the breakfast cereal in an unusual place. (I don't remember which sugar-based cereal was hosting the contest, but I do remember my sister and I failing to persuade our mother to let us accompany her to church one Sunday morning carrying a bowlful.) Next came the proof of purchase. Along with the entry, the competition required entrants to cut out and collect tokens printed on the product packaging. Larger packets had more tokens, encouraging maximum consumption. Finally there was the tiebreaker. In no more than ten words, write down why you love Golden Nuggets or Shreddies or Rice Krispies or whatever.

Describing why you like something in a few words takes effort. My younger, naive self was convinced that if I won, it would be *my* carefully considered response used as the brand's next marketing campaign. Not any longer. I can now see those breakfast cereal competitions for what they really were. A masterclass in influence and persuasion. Arrange for thousands of kids to pester their parents to buy breakfast cereal, get them to think carefully about, and then write down, why they like the product and then post it to the manufacturer. All for a close-to-zero chance of winning a bike.

As an influence strategy, it's genius.

The brilliance of the breakfast cereal competition strategy is founded on the principle of commitment and consistency. Once people make an initial commitment, particularly a voluntary one that requires effort, they encounter a personal and an interpersonal psychological pressure to remain consistent with that commitment. We do this for reasons that extend way beyond bowls of snap, crackle and pop. Acting consistently allows us to feel good about ourselves, satisfying the fundamental motivation of ego. Not only that. People who live up to their commitments are afforded a desirable standing in the groups they belong to. They are seen as more dependable, reliable and trustworthy – attributes that are not only helpful at work but also in life more generally.

The principle of commitment and consistency is a powerful tool in the armoury of anyone seeking to persuade others. The key for the persuader is to start small and seek relatively minor initial commitments from those they want to get on board. When researchers posing as road traffic safety officials went door to door asking householders if they would place a large sign on the front of their property with the words "Drive carefully", few complied. But one area bucked the trend with homeowners significantly more likely to agree to this unappealing request. Maybe it was a neighbourhood of families with young children who were understandably motivated to support calls for safer roads, so their kids can play on the streets and ride their bikes. Or perhaps a recent accident or near-miss focused minds on the importance of road safety. But neither of these reasons was responsible for people agreeing to such a large commitment. It was something else entirely. The previous week, some homeowners had been asked to place a postcard in the window of their car signalling their support for the campaign. This small, voluntary act served as the initial commitment. When later asked to support the campaign by allowing the installation of a much larger sign, they agreed because the bigger request was entirely consistent with their earlier, smaller commitment.

Start small and build

Another example where a small initial commitment influenced a larger future action comes from a 2012 study I carried out with Rupert Dunbar-Rees and Suraj Bassi, two medical doctors.[26] Our goal was simple. Reduce the number of patients who made appointments in healthcare centres and GP surgeries but failed to attend. In one study we instructed receptionists to ask patients to repeat back the time and date of their appointment they had been given. This verbal commitment yielded an admittedly small but still welcome return. Those who confirmed their appointment verbally were 3% less likely to no-show. However, in keeping with the breakfast cereal and road safety examples, we measured a much bigger effect when we asked patients to make not just a verbal commitment, but also an active and effortful one. Noticing that receptionists often write down appointment details on a reminder card and give it to the patient, we suggested the receptionists hand over the blank card for the patient to write down the time and date themselves. Missed appointments dropped by 18%.

A similar no-show challenge emerged during the coronavirus pandemic with many facing lockdowns and being forced to work from home. Fast internet speeds and online meeting apps meant it was possible to conduct a lot of business virtually, so many organisations and companies adopted webinars as a tool for sales and networking. They quickly learned that a potential customer *signing up* to an online webinar was not the same as a potential customer *turning up* to an online webinar. Some reported as many as three-quarters of people who registered to attend a webinar would fail to attend. A firm's reputation, status in the market and the recruiting of expert speakers can contribute to better turnouts. So too can the use of the commitment and consistency principle. One financial institution found it could stem the tide of audience attrition by asking those who registered to attend one of their webinars to submit a question they would be interested in hearing the guest speaker answer. This simple commitment reduced no-show rates, often by as much as half.

Several important insights emerge for anyone struggling to persuade people to get on board with an idea and then follow through on their commitments and promises. The first concerns the importance of others' participation. As tempting as it is to do the work ourselves – if only to ensure things get done – this can result in the influencer becoming more committed to the idea than the people they are seeking to engage and influence. Seeking small, voluntary and effortful commitments early in the process of change becomes crucial because they create a context for people's preference for consistency to flow.

Another concerns the importance of commitments being made publicly. In one study householders were asked if they were willing to make energy efficiencies in their home and were given a list of energy-saving tips. Unfortunately good intentions and good advice weren't enough to change habits. But when the researchers asked another group of householders about their willingness to make energy efficiencies, gave the same saving advice and promised to publish their names on a list of public-spirited, energy-efficient households, the effect was immediate. Many more households reduced their energy use.[27]

It would appear that three things should be uppermost in any influencer's mind when seeking to evaluate whether any tacit commitment secured will turn into a subsequent and meaningful action. First, is the commitment a voluntary one? Second, does the person or group now have an effortful action to undertake? Third, and most crucially, who else knows?

I can't credibly claim that securing a voluntary, effortful and public commitment will always result in change. But I am confident without one, your influence is unlikely to be realised.

Consistency at work

- For reasons of ego and positive social identity, people are motivated to live up to their commitments and self-ascribed traits.

- Aligning proposals and propositions to an audience's previously stated commitments and values can increase the attractiveness of your proposition.

- Master persuaders seek initial, voluntary and effortful commitments from others and seek to make them public.

Principle 7. Scarcity

People want more of the things they can have less of

There are various ways to measure the popularity of a British royal wedding. Online and television viewing figures is an obvious one. So too is the number of spectators lining parade routes, often days in advance to secure the best viewpoint. Sales of bunting, Union Flag hats and commemorative souvenirs, is another. By this last metric the marriage in April 2005 of the Prince of Wales (now King Charles III) to Camilla Parker Bowles was not a universally embraced affair. Shops in central London and the royal town of Windsor reported slow sales of tea towels, coffee mugs and other wedding-related memorabilia. But things changed a few days before the wedding, with increasing numbers of shoppers scurrying to buy royal knick-knacks and collectables. Did a sudden warming of hearts towards the betrothed couple prompt this sudden rush? Possibly. But it's more likely that sales received a boost because of the death of Pope John Paul II a week earlier. To allow the then Prince of Wales to attend the funeral as a representative of the Queen, Buckingham Palace announced that the royal wedding would be postponed by a day. Souvenir stores suddenly found themselves with stock featuring the wrong date.

Spotting an opportunity, some started buying up these wrong-dated souvenirs. Several journalists already in Windsor to cover the royal event asked shoppers leaving stores with bags of souvenirs whether they were supporters of the royal family. Most said no. The motivation to purchase royal mementos had little to do with the royal wedding. They simply thought that the misdated items would be rarer and, consequently, worth more in the future.

The rule of the rare

Most people succumb to wanting more of what they can have less of. When we learn that the availability of something is dwindling, supplies are scarce or opportunities are accessible for only a limited time, our desire for them often rises, along with a potential willingness to pay more. Think Beanie Babies™, Football Collector cards, the Hermès Birkin bag and certain smartphones.

Interestingly, it's not necessary for something to be genuinely scarce for it to exert an influence. Sometimes the perception that something might be scarce is all that's needed. A good example was seen during the coronavirus pandemic. In the early days of lockdown, rumours spread of supermarkets experiencing high demand for certain everyday items including pasta, hand sanitiser and toilet rolls. With these rumours came the inevitable demand, leading to the irrational purchase of stocks far above what people needed. Very often it wasn't the lack of stocks themselves that drove scarcity but the resultant run on products whose availability was generally good until the rumours started. Toilet paper was arguably one of the more problematic products to be the subject of perceptions of this scarcity – not because of matters of hygiene, but size. Unlike pasta or soup, whose scarcity leaves relatively small spaces on shelves, a lack of toilet paper creates a whole aisle of emptiness. Shoppers seeing a barren wilderness in the bathroom tissue aisle could be forgiven for thinking Armageddon was imminent and, in response, began purchasing excessive stocks of other staples, falsely fuelling further the perception of scarcity of other products.

There are several reasons why scarcity of an item or opportunity, whether real or rumoured, drives us to want it more. We have already explored one – people's aversion to loss – in Chapter 5. However, it is worth reminding ourselves that framing a message in terms of what someone might lose is often more persuasive than the same message delivered as a gain. There's a common saying in the financial services industry that is as entertaining as it is instructive. "Phone a client at 4am and tell them if they act now, they'll make twenty grand; the client will fire you. But phone a client at 4am and tell them if they *fail* to act now, they'll lose twenty grand; you'll have a customer for life." Notice in this scenario that the client and the amount are the same. The only thing that changes is whether attention focuses on the gain or on the loss.

People are also influenced by scarcity because of the general inclination to respond unfavourably to restrictions on our freedoms. We can all recall, as teenagers, the nervous thrill of being served in a bar or watching an 18-rated film. We can also recall how that thrill waned considerably on our coming of age. Our reaction to restrictions is one reason why product manufacturers of cars, kitchens, phones and so on produce limited or special editions; they understand the magnetic attraction of a unique feature or a limited edition. It also explains why supermarkets report increased sales of a product when they limit supplies to a maximum of two items per customer – despite knowing only too well that most customers ordinarily only ever purchase one.

The implications for influencers and communicators should be clear. If your proposal or proposition has a feature or attribute that is genuinely unique or scarce, then ensure it is made prominent to your audience. Similarly, to increase your colleagues' engagement on work projects and initiatives, point to the scarcity of the opportunity. "It's not often we get the chance to be involved in programmes like this." And in situations where you have a genuine opportunity for messages that convey a limited time ("Sale ends Friday") or a limited number ("Only 10 units remaining"), the advice is to employ the latter.

As well as features and attributes, it can be influential to frame certain kinds of information as scarce. In one study, wholesale beef buyers more than doubled their orders when they were informed that a shortage of Australian beef was likely because of forecasted bad weather. But when those purchasers were also informed that the information came from an exclusive source that was not available to others, they increased their orders six-fold. Not only were beef supplies scarce; the information that beef was scarce was also scarce.[28] Importantly, it was also true. So, in situations where you have information that is new and exclusive, and assuming that you are free to do so, share it early with those who could benefit.

Scarcity at work

- Opportunities appear more valuable when they are less available or when availability is dwindling.

- Make prominent information about your proposal that is either genuinely rare or that comes from an exclusive source.

- Limited-number offers are more persuasive than limited-time ones.

8

The practice of influence

In the 20 or so years I have been studying, writing about and teaching the psychology of influence and persuasion, I've lost count of the number of questions I have been asked by people interested in convincing others to say "yes" to them more often. Certainly hundreds; maybe thousands. But one question has emerged as by far the most common.

"What one thing can I do that will immediately make me more persuasive?"

I quickly learned that the factually correct answer to this question was something few people wanted to hear. That's because there is no one-size-fits-all approach to convincing others. Influencing and persuading others, as the Influence Equation suggests, can be a complex, often dynamic process requiring the right combination of evidence, economics and emotions while also taking account of the context and specific situation. When explaining this I noticed that some people's eyes would glaze over. Our reductionist way of life, it seems, is not suited to explaining philosophies, premises and principles. What people really wanted was a simple, immediately actionable hack that would help. So, I gave them one. "The best way to increase your persuasiveness", I would reply, "is to inject some humanity into your requests."

I was surprised at how many people seemed satisfied

with this answer. Some even thanked me before setting off, presumably in pursuit of another sought-after nugget that promised further improvement in their busy lives. But not everyone. Others saw the problem with the "What one thing?" question, recognising how vague and untethered from reality seeking a single catch-all answer is, and how unhelpful the answer is likely to be.

These were the people likely to ask a more specific question. In this chapter I tackle ten of the most popular ones. So consider this chapter a question-and-answer (or agony aunt) session in book form, offering up what I hope will be useful and usable advice for some of the more common influence challenges many of us will face.

*

1. *Part of my job requires me to provide quotes, write proposals and negotiate with potential customers. My team and I often debate, when discussing prices, whether it is better to make the opening offer or wait for the other side to show their hand. What is the right answer?*

There is no right answer, but there are certainly a few insights that should help. I once heard a businessperson describe the first few minutes of a negotiation as like the opening minutes of a boxing match. People dance around, reluctant to throw the first punch (i.e. make the opening offer) because they worry that doing so might lose them a competitive advantage. But according to persuasion science, rather than wait for your opponent to make the opening offer, you are likely to be much better off if you go first. All else being equal, this rule holds true regardless of whether you are the buyer or the seller.

In a series of negotiation simulations, agents representing a factory sale agreed to an average sale price of $24.8m if they made the first offer. However, if they waited for buyers to make their offer first, the average selling price fell to $19.7m. The primary reason concerns what is known as an *anchor* which subtly influences subsequent discussions. Initial anchors, even arbitrary ones, frequently bind people to positions they find hard to move away from. For example, one study asked people to estimate the cost of a bottle of wine. Before volunteering a price, they were asked to randomly select a ball from a bag where half the balls were numbered 90 and the other half were numbered 10. Those picking the balls with the number 90 estimated the value of the wine as much higher.[1] It is a useful reminder of how, even though we know we should determine the value of something independent of any initial offer, we often find it hard to move away sufficiently from the first number tabled.

But what if you get beaten to the first punch? The advice is to prepare a written list of why your price is justified before going into any negotiation. Having this in front of you can be a helpful tool to counter the possibility that you begin questioning the accuracy of your own judgement after hearing your opponent's opening offer.

2. *Any other tips on negotiations?*

Two. The first concerns precision. Malia Mason, a professor at Columbia Business School, suggests one way to boost the outcome of any negotiation is to avoid rounding up or down your offers. When people see a precise number, they tend to assume there is a specific and legitimate reason why, and are subsequently less inclined to question them. They also tend to be more conciliatory when countering.

In one of Mason's studies buyers interested in purchasing a second-hand car received one of three asking prices: £2,000, £1,865 or £2,135. They were then asked to respond with an offer of their own. Those who saw an asking price with a precise ending countered with an offer that was, on average, 10% less than what was asked. But those who saw the rounded price countered with an offer that was 23% less. The precise asking price resulted in a higher final selling price, even when it was less than the rounded price.[2] So when the time comes to sell the rusting Ford on your driveway you might end up with more cash if you advertise a selling price of £1,927 rather than a straight £2,000. And if you happen to be in the market for an old banger, I advise paying special attention to sellers whose opening demands are uncharacteristically specific.

A second insight concerns not how you negotiate, but where. As any sports supporter will tell you, all else being equal, teams who play on home soil tend to have an edge over their visiting opponents. A series of studies published in the journal *Organizational Behavior and Human Decision Processes* suggest the same might be true when it comes to doing business deals.[3] Negotiators were recruited to bargain on a series of contracts where one was assigned the role of purchaser and the other the supplier. As you might imagine, a considerable part of the negotiation centred on price, with purchasers wanting to pay as little as possible and suppliers wanting the opposite. But one of the negotiators was also assigned "home" office status where their name and company logo was prominently displayed, they could choose which chair to sit in, display details of company relevant activities on a whiteboard and even have the key to the office. Dealmakers assigned "away" status were asked to wait in a temporary location until the home team was ready to receive them.

Like sports teams, conferring a home advantage led to better outcomes for negotiators, regardless of whether they were purchasers and sellers. When it comes to being a persuasive negotiator the researchers claim that location can make a difference, probably because a familiar space boosts confidence whereas negotiating in unfamiliar territory reduces it. So next time you need to negotiate, inviting people to your location might boost your chances of a good deal. Who you are, it would seem, is often a function of where you are.

3. *There is a ghastly person at work who is argumentative and two-faced and frequently belittles or even outright dismisses anything that isn't their idea. The problem is they are respected by management and carry a lot of weight. How can I build a working relationship with someone I neither like nor want to work with?*

I remember someone once spending a significant part of an evening out complaining about an obnoxious, stubborn and uncooperative colleague at work. Other words were used too but are unsuitable for print. To be fair, the alcohol probably didn't help. As the evening progressed, the consumption of red wine only served to pour more fuel on their fire of loathing. A casual enquiry that surely there was *something* likeable about this person only prompted another tirade.

We can all sympathise. Many of us will encounter someone we have to work with who we would prefer not to. The problem is that no matter how mollifying it might be to deride and disparage them, come tomorrow you still face the challenge of deciding how to work with them to get the job done.

Persuasion researchers have identified a potential strategy that can be effective and is also somewhat counter-intuitive. Find something likeable about the individual you dislike and tell them. I realise this is easier said than done. Most people find it easier to generate reasons that support their current point of view rather than oppose it. But as you often have little choice about who you work with, the advice is to follow a two-step approach.

The first is to recognise that, despite what we may think or have been told, everyone has at least one redeeming quality or characteristic. Someone somewhere does like that person. Your job is to locate that redeeming quality or characteristic, remembering that it doesn't necessarily have to be a personal feature. Something about their approach to work, their success on a previous project or their commitment to the cause can suffice. Second, having identified a likeable feature, you need to find a way of communicating this to the person. Choose your moment carefully. Do it privately and if the thought of doing this makes you retch, consider telling someone connected to you both who is likely to pass the message on.

Executed authentically this "charm and disarm" strategy might provide an additional upside. By focusing on an admirable feature in someone you find difficult to deal with, you might actually end up warming to them a little more – and they, you.

4. *I have recently been promoted at work and now have people who report to me. I am dreading review time when I might have to deliver negative feedback and bad news. Any tips?*

Feedback, both good and bad, is an inescapable part of life at work and home. Waiting to learn whether we achieved a promotion, won that new client or have been chosen to be part of the exciting new project everyone is talking about can be a rollercoaster of emotions from hope to dread, elation to despair. It's certainly no picnic for the givers of news either, especially when what needs to be delivered is anything but rosy. Even when you have nothing to do with the cause of the unfortunate news itself and are merely the messenger, it is hard to avoid being tarnished by it.

Classic managerial textbooks advocate a three-stage approach. First, prepare the recipient to receive the bad news by outlining the evidence that led up to the decision. Second, the delivery of the feedback itself. Third is "shoring", defined as an attempt to dilute the sting of any sorry news with empathetic phrases like "It's not as bad as you think" and generally playing up the positives.

I am not completely convinced by the effectiveness of this bad-news-softened-by-good-news approach, primarily because it depends whether you are asking the recipient or the giver of the news. When asked "Do you want the good news first, or the bad?", recipients typically want the bad news first. Perhaps they think once the negative feedback is out of the way, the conversation might end on a lighter, more positive note. Deliverers of bad news, however, frequently think the opposite. Presumably they believe that by saying something positive at the start, they increase the chances of being liked and insulate themselves from incurring any personal or social costs when they do serve up the unfortunate news.

It doesn't take a genius to see that the main beneficiary of the "s**t sandwich" is the deliverer of negative feedback. So I would advise thinking about the optimal outcome. If your primary goal is to shield any negative emotional reaction, then relay the bad news first. But if, as a manager or supervisor, the purpose of delivering negative feedback is to influence some change in the recipient, it might be best to end with the bad news. Just make sure that any negative news is accompanied by a specific and realistic plan of what can be done to address or correct the situation.

5. *With virtual and hybrid working a common feature of working life, what advice do you have for influencing others when I am on a screen rather than physically present?*

My team and I are asked about this a lot. How can someone have influence and impact when the ability to shake people by the hand, look them in the eye and engage socially is absent? It's a fair question now that hybrid ways of working have become the norm. Whether you are attempting to win over a prospect, negotiate a pay rise or build a business network, it's tougher from behind a screen. But not impossible. Here are a few things to bear in mind.

Camera etiquette is important. After switching to online teaching during the lockdown, someone at my university had the good sense to send out stickers of eyes to place above our cameras. This anthropomorphising helps because it focuses attention on looking directly into the camera which can be taxing when your screen is populated by dozens of postage stamp size faces.

Be aware of volume variance. Many people raise their voice when speaking online or over the phone. Studies conducted during the pandemic suggest that people, on average, speak 15% louder on Zoom and Teams than when talking face to face.[4] The virtual world doesn't allow for immediate calibration. It's better to turn down your microphone and people can ask you to speak louder if necessary, than the other way round.

The virtual interaction also lacks the ability to show that we are listening, which is crucial for influence. Waiters and waitresses who mimic their customers by repeating their order using exactly the same words can increase their tips by as much as 70%.[5] Why? Because mimicry increases our sense of closeness and being understood by another. The strategy appears to be effective in virtual settings too. Studies show that the matching of language patterns is especially effective when used in the early parts of video calls, but less effective at the end. The advice is to write down key words you hear someone use during the initial exchanges and say them back to the other person as a means of creating a more influential connection.

Finally, avoid narcissistic tendencies. We might juggle a host of other activities – writing emails, taking in the weekly shop and scolding the kids – while simultaneously believing the person on our screen is wholly dedicated and paying attention to us. They're probably not. So think reciprocity. If you want someone to focus their attention on you, focus your attention on them first. And remember, however efficient email and videos are, they are bloodless. So maybe ditch the keyboard and screen for your next interaction and pick up the phone or meet in the office instead.

6. *As a project manager I often struggle to keep people on track with tasks. Programmes and initiatives can fall behind schedule or stall completely, and I find myself constantly chasing people, which I'm sure influences what they think of me. Any ideas on how I can nudge people along and still remain liked?*

It's tempting to hope that your success at convincing people to get on board with an idea will be enough to keep them engaged and see a project through to the end. But persuasion and persistence are not the same, so it is important to have a few strategies up your sleeve when motivation wanes and you need to refocus efforts. Sushi restaurants and marathon runners offer some helpful tips.

Ayelet Fishbach is a psychologist and leading expert on motivation. She finds people's enthusiasm to finish a task is boosted when they focus on the smaller amount of progress they have made towards its completion, rather than the larger amount of effort that remains. Psychologists call this shifting of attention the small-area principle.

In one of Fishbach's studies, some customers in a sushi restaurant received a card with ten blank spaces and earned a stamp each time they bought lunch. A completed card could be exchanged for a free meal. Another set of customers received an already completed card and a stamp was removed every time they made a purchase. Those who accumulated stamps returned to the restaurant to make further purchases almost twice as quickly as those who had stamps taken away.[6] This makes sense. An action that takes us from 10% task completion to 20% is a doubling of progress. Moving from 70% to 80% is proportionally much less. But at the half-way point the emphasis shifts. When marathon runners reach the 13-mile stage of a race, their internal dialogue changes. Instead of counting up the miles run, they start to count down the distance remaining.

Given people's tendency to stay motivated when their focus is directed to the small area, project managers should provide reports and updates that highlight whichever is the smaller number: progress made or progress remaining. In the early stages you should say: "You are already 20% of the way towards the goal," not: "You have 80% to go." When the half-way mark is passed, shift language to: "Only 20% left to go," rather than: "You're 80% of the way there."

Sales managers might find this focusing on the small area a useful way to keep staff motivated towards reaching sales and performance targets. "One week in and you have already achieved 15% of your quarterly target." But as they get closer to the target: "Only 10% of your target left."

7. *At my last review I received feedback that, although I am often the most knowledgeable person in the room, I'm not seen as very persuasive. My manager says I need to be more charismatic. Is that even possible?*

You are in good company. Despite his undeniable genius, Albert Einstein was never considered an inspiring communicator. His lectures often attracted audiences of one-digit numbers. Rumour was, after one particularly poor showing, the university cancelled his class entirely. Like many people, Einstein found that good knowledge and good delivery are not the same; those who lack the magic sauce of charisma often go unfairly ignored.

The *Oxford Dictionary* defines charisma as "a compelling attractiveness or charm that can inspire devotion in others". Colourful descriptions like these aren't helpful because they tend to throw up more questions. What inspires devotion? How do you achieve presence? What, exactly, is a compelling attractiveness? Psychological research is more useful and highlights three important ingredients to charisma.

The first, surgency, is the ability to express an idea with energy and positivity. How? It seems hand movements are important. Using clever software a team of researchers turned videos of TED talk speakers into animated stick figures which were then shown to audiences without sound. The animations that used more hand movements were judged as being more energetic and enthusiastic. More importantly, audiences accurately predicted the amount of applause the various stick speakers received in real life: those predisposed to passionate gesticulation gained more applause. Other studies have found that the most popular TED talks are typically made by presenters who use almost twice as many hand gestures as less popular speakers speaking on the same topic. Hand movements act as a "second language" that reveals cues about a communicator's perceived charisma. They literally signal a messenger's genuine feeling for an issue or situation. Second, charismatic people use more analogies and anecdotes, which ties in well with the chapter on emotions. Finally, charismatic folks tend to be better at thinking on their feet.

Charisma is unlikely to be an ability that people are born with, but a set of skills and traits that can be learned. A good starting point is to use more analogies and anecdotes in presentations and appeals. Persuasion isn't something that happens only in the mind; it happens in the hands, too.

8. It's obvious that the words we use really do matter when it comes to influencing others. But are there any words that are particularly attractive to audiences? And what words should I avoid using?

In 1974, an American psychologist named Elizabeth Loftus became famous for her studies into the power of words. In one experiment she showed people a short film of a road traffic accident before asking them to guess how fast the cars were travelling.[7] Some were asked: "What speed do you think the car was going when it bumped into the vehicle in front?" For others, the word "bumped" was replaced with "collided", "hit" or "smashed". People estimated the car to be travelling much faster when the words "hit" or "smashed" were used, despite the video being the same. This is no trivial matter. Speed is important when it comes to assessing damages. Judges typically award higher damages to victims and convict culprits for longer.

Loftus's early experiments reveal the important role words play in the persuasion process. Words don't serve just as a means of communication, but also as tools wielded to effect influence. Sometimes it's not the word itself that caries sway but its form, with one study demonstrating that nouns can trump verbs when it comes to persuading people to take action. After Harvard University's Todd Rodgers asked US citizens how important it was to be a voter, more people turned up at polling booths than the number asked how important it was to vote.[8] The increase in turnout was enough to swing a closely fought election, demonstrating that words don't only persuade individuals; they can also influence and shape whole societies.

Tense matters too. Research shows that online reviews are

often seen as more credible when written in the present tense rather than the past tense, suggesting that online influencers could benefit by encouraging their followers to post more temporally sensitive appraisals. Bricks and mortar businesses can profit too. Restaurants should ask customers to post reviews that explicitly mentions a point in time as close to the present as possible: for example, a sentence such as: "We just got back from this restaurant" or: "My partner and I visited today."

Interestingly, there is one frequently used word that studies suggest should be used with more care. It is the word "new". As appealing and attractive as it might sound to some, for many the word comes with an array of potentially less compelling associations; untested, inexperienced, not yet mainstream. Of course, should your proposition target the kinds of people who consider themselves innovative thinkers and early adopters, then "new" could fit the bill perfectly. But because most people don't act that way, caution is advised.

9. *I am part of a large multinational company and I work with colleagues from various countries. What influence strategies work well when persuading people from cultures different to my own?*

Influence is a global pursuit, so it makes sense to consider the bearing cultural origins can have on how we persuade, and how we are persuaded. Three things come to mind.

The first can be described as preparing the ground. Scientific research has shown what most people are already intuitively aware of. Those who live and work in ethnically and culturally diverse groups generally find it easier to identify with the broad range of characteristics that make up humanity. Members of these diverse groups tend to be more helpful and considerate to the requests of others. But the spread of this kind of culturally inclusive environment cannot be left to chance. Managers need to take the lead in ensuring that new recruits are exposed to the diversity of personalities at work in the form of early and frequent contact. It's hard work, but effort will frequently be rewarded in the form of a helpful side-effect: increased trust. Recall, in Chapter 4, that managers who initiate, maintain and encourage frequent social exchanges are not only rated as more likeable and productive but are also considered more trustworthy and therefore more influential. This applies not just within their own cultural in-groups but also extends to others.

A second point to consider concerns similarities. Recall Cialdini's principle of liking, which describes people's predisposition to favour requests that come from those they see as similar to themselves. Some might be concerned that this preference for similarity risks undermining an organisation's cultural diversity, resulting in group members only helping their own. But it is worth noting research that demonstrates that similarities of race and ethnicity are frequently crowded out by similarities of beliefs and values. Therefore, highlighting how your request is aligned with a commonly held value or belief should provide a helpful context for influence, especially in situations where you are attempting to persuade someone over whom you have no little or no positional power.

Third, consider some country-specific dynamics for influence at work. One study conducted in a large global banking group sought to determine the factors that would persuade someone from one culture to assist a co-worker from another culture on a task for which they would be neither rewarded nor recognised. In individualistic cultures like the United States, the UK and Canada, people were most likely to be persuaded by somebody who had previously done something for them. Not the case in collective countries like China, Indonesia and Japan. Here requests were more likely to be granted if the influencer was connected to someone in their department, particularly someone of high rank. In Mediterranean and South American cultures, requests were more likely to be granted when they came from a messenger connected to the target's family or friends. And in Germanic and Scandinavian cultures, persuasion attempts were most successful when the persuader pointed out that their request was consistent with the organisation's official rules and policies.[9]

10. *I am a customer service manager and admit that our levels of service have fallen in recent years because of cutbacks. What can we do to influence perceptions more positively?*

The number one piece of advice is to make sure that customer experiences end well, no matter how badly (or well) they started.

Most people have encountered an otherwise positive experience being ruined by something untoward that happened at the end. A lovely evening out at a restaurant with friends, spoiled because the waiter spilled coffee on someone's lap. An idyllic holiday tainted because of a cancelled return flight, resulting in a long wait with tired, irritated youngsters on uncomfortable airport seats. It's not the experience itself that is ruined. The joyous meal and laughter around the table doesn't change. Neither does the restful, well-deserved week in the sun. What gets ruined is our recollection of those experiences because memories are etched into our minds with extremity and recency. People tend to remember the peak moment of pain or pleasure in an experience and what happens at the end. Almost all our other memories of that experience get crowded out by these two moments.

Termed the "peak-end" phenomenon, it provided a helpful insight to an executive who once called me to talk about a frustrating and increasingly damaging situation for his business – a portfolio of UK campsites with fancy self-catering cabins.[10] Shortly after the covid-19 lockdown rules were relaxed, business was booming for campsites and caravan parks. The promise of an outdoor, self-sufficient break offered a viable alternative for families keen to avoid the hassle of confusing travel rules, restricted flights and costly re-entry tests. He explained how customers, as they left the parks for the drive home, would frequently report what a surprisingly fun time they had. Spotting an opportunity, the executive wisely asked his delighted customers to post an online review when they got home. Many did. He was surprised, however, at how lukewarm many of these reviews were. Those who offered glowing reports to him and his staff on leaving the park, seemed to experience a change of heart a week or two later. "I don't understand what's happening," he remarked frustratingly. "Between leaving us with wide-eyed smiles and them writing their review their minds change. Did they mix us up with another campsite?"

A couple of carefully placed questions soon got to the crux. The increased patronage at the parks had led to growing demands on housekeeping staff who, in an effort to speed up the turnaround of cabins, asked vacating guests to strip their beds, gather up the linens and towels and return them to the housekeeping station. This became the last thing that guests, who had otherwise had a fabulous time, remembered. Consequently, it loomed large in their memories weeks later when writing their review. It is easy to imagine an otherwise happy customer docking a star or two from their rating as a result. There was a simple fix for the park: provide linen packs on entry for guests to make their beds, rather than asking them to strip all the beds on departure. It made sure that people left happy and unencumbered by memories of last-minute laundry duties.

When it comes to influencing customers' memories of their experiences with your company or business, the advice is to pay careful attention to the final stages of client interactions and make sure they end on a high. I'm not suggesting this is an excuse to worry less about how good the service is before then, but this shift in focus can help when dealing with exchanges that didn't get off to the best start.

9

Influencing (ethically) at work

No one will know for sure whether Henry Wells turned in his grave. But the news, in September 2016, that the bank he had set up a century and a half previously was complicit in a fraud spanning 14 years and affecting more than 3 million customers might well have given him cause to.

Wells was a principled man. The son of a Presbyterian minister, his humble beginnings as an apprentice shoemaker, coupled with a desire to help others, probably contributed to his moral character. As a young man he travelled the eastern cities of the United States seeking ways to lessen the noticeable stammer and verbal tic he had suffered since his early years. After finding a successful method, he made a point of freely passing on his techniques to others who suffered similar speech impediments. It was around this time that he met William Fargo and, later, a stagecoach driver named John Butterfield. Together they set up a messaging firm founded on honour and principle. They called it the American Express Company. Yes, *that* American Express. The company prided itself on delivering packages promptly and conveying communiqués accurately. Later, the men turned their attention to the burgeoning Californian Gold Rush and established Wells Fargo. It went on to become one of America's most trusted banking businesses.

But long and hard-earned trust is quickly lost. The 2016

scandal cost Wells Fargo dearly. The bank was ordered to pay billions of dollars in a series of record-breaking penalties and settlements based on an ill-advised employee incentive programme designed to persuade customers to sign up for banking services they neither wanted nor needed. Egged on by senior executives who allegedly urged employees to "Go for Gr-Eight" by selling eight products to each customer, millions of savings accounts and credit cards accounts were opened fraudulently without consent. Investors and customers, outraged at the bank's behaviour and loss of reputation, sold stock and closed accounts.

Yet despite the costly implications, unethical practices like these are not rare. Enron, an energy company, engaged in accounting fraud which led to its bankruptcy. Car manufacturer Volkswagen installed "defeat devices" in its diesel vehicles to manipulate emissions tests. In the aftermath, sales dropped to a sixteenth of their average levels and the company's favourable reputation rating swung from plus 70% to minus 80%.[1] Executives and officials at FIFA, football's governing body, were involved in a widespread corruption accepting bribes in exchange for votes on where tournaments would be held and the awarding of lucrative broadcasting rights. Its reputation has yet to recover.

Invariably, institutional malfeasances begin with individuals. Elizabeth Holmes, the founder of Theranos, hoodwinked her entire company into marshalling behind a revolutionary blood-testing technology later revealed to be flawed and inaccurate. Duped investors, bruised employees and a mistrusting public fought back with charges of industrial fraud, deception and conspiracy. Vijay Eswaran, the founder of QuestNet, created a multi-level marketing scam comprising misleading sales techniques and false promises all based on an illegal pyramid scheme. Legal actions and country-wide bans quickly followed. And former Goldman Sachs director Rajat Gupta leaked confidential information about the organisation's insider dealings to hedge fund managers who used the information to make profitable trades. He was sentenced to two years in prison and ordered to pay $5m in fines.

It is worth pondering why scandals like these keep happening. Surely the sizeable financial penalties meted out by the courts are enough of a deterrent, not to mention the reputational damage. In the United States, a Securities and Exchange Commission study of almost 600 firms found that companies whose misconduct is made public subsequently lose, on average, 40% of their market value.[2] In surveys, eight out of ten consumers agree with the statement: "a company's ethicality directly influences my purchase decisions". Yet unethical practices, whilst by no means the norm, still regularly prevail.

EY, a consulting firm, has conducted research suggesting that this is not an issue of awareness.[3] Its investigations show that the overwhelming majority of businesses, as well as the people working in them, are more than cognisant of the reputational price they could pay should any unethical practices be outed. Yet some seem willing to chance their arm anyway. Why? Many factors are at play, but two seem particularly important. The first is simple economics. If the potential rewards outweigh the risk of getting caught, then inevitably some will take a risk. The second concerns self-persuasion. Many who commit unethical acts seem able to convince themselves they won't ever get caught.

*

The ability to influence others is foundational to success.

At the same time it is a practice laden with moral dilemma. The fact that we can persuade others by the way we present evidence, structure an incentive and activate specific emotions – all without needing to change the core of our message – is appealing. Particularly if it speeds up the process of change. Expedience and urgency are unlikely to go out of fashion anytime soon. Yet, without due diligence, the cost of winning today's argument might be an unwanted price paid tomorrow, either in the form of a financial cost or a moral regret. Or both.

These potential repercussions might be the reason why some people believe that all influence is manipulative and therefore has no place in their repertoire of skills. But this thinking also raises a challenge. Without influence there is no change. An environment lacking in persuasion is one also lacking in progress. Doing nothing might be an attractive proposition in theory, but in practice influence has no antonym. To do nothing is to do something. To ignore or choose not to participate is, in itself, an influence strategy. When it comes to its practice, we are all either complicit in the influence process or swept along by it.

Christine Clavien, an ethicist at the University of Geneva, suggests that the practice of influence can be categorised in terms of three approaches.[4]

- The *target-driven influence*, or *better for others* approach, which advocates that the sole focus of the communicator should be on helping others.
- The *better for the persuader* approach, which is entirely self-serving and venal and designed to serve solely the influencer's own interests.
- The *social approach*, which advocates influence strategies that strive to make everything better for everyone.

Models like this neatly summarise the options available

to those who want to influence others with the assumption (and perhaps I'm being naïve here) that most land on the third approach, where their strategies make things better for all concerned. But categorising influence approaches is not the same as applying them. Nor do they consider who or what is doing the persuading: an institution or an organisation, or an individual operating on their behalf or alone.

Fortunately, there are frameworks and checklists in existence that can help. Here are two. The first is designed primarily for organisations and the second for individuals, although they clearly share a common sentiment and spirit.

Influencing ethically for organisations

Most organisations and institutions strive to behave in responsible and ethical ways, recognising the importance and advantages of prioritising a principled and honourable approach to doing business. Many will have ethics boards whose remit is to ensure worthy conduct. Others routinely include discussions about ethical standards as an agenda item during board meetings. Most, however, are likely to discuss matters of ethicality and principle on an ad hoc basis, usually when a potential issue or possible risk arises. Regardless of how these conversations and debates come about, it can be helpful to have frameworks and checklists to guide discussions and offer guardrails providing for healthy and instructive challenge and debate. Many frameworks and checklists are freely available. One worth noting was developed by my behavioural scientist colleague Olivia Pattison, called TRUST.[5]

Pattison's TRUST framework comprises five factors (Truth, Respect, Uncontestable, Spillovers and Transparency) that boards and teams can consider when reviewing their business practices and ways of working through an ethical lens.

Truth. *Are your business practices, products and procedures grounded in truth?*

Although Pattison acknowledges that the concept of truth is subjective, she maintains that a healthy business acts in the spirit of truth and honesty, ensuring that it behaves in ways that customers, colleagues and the wider community are not being deliberately misled or deceived by its policies, practices and products.

Respect. *Does your business practice respect freedom of choice and individual agency?*

Pattison believes that institutions and businesses should respect and preserve people's freedom of choice and agency. Organisational interests, particularly those relating to financial and commercial activities, should, where appropriate and possible, minimise any likelihood of disenfranchisement, as when certain options become difficult or more costly for certain groups to choose or acquire. An example of a business failing the respect factor is a company that offers preferential rates only to new customers or subscribers, while long-term customers and patrons pay more for the same. Similarly, organisations that make it difficult for current customers to cancel services and subscriptions, a concept that *Nudge* authors Richard Thaler and Cass Sunstein call *sludge*, also fail on Pattison's respect mark.[6]

Uncontestable. *Are you comfortable defending your practice in public?*

"Murder cannot be hid long; ... at the length truth will out," said Lancelot Gobbo in Shakespeare's tale of retribution, *The Merchant of Venice*. It is a sentiment that might equally be applied to business, despite EY's research suggesting many executives believe unethical behaviour is likely to go undetected. Pattison's

TRUST framework encourages organisations to scrutinise their policies and practices carefully to the extent they could defend them satisfactorily if they were ever challenged.

Spillovers. *Have you considered the potential consequences, unintended or otherwise?*

No one can be totally sure that a policy or business strategy implemented today will not have consequences in the future, potentially causing harm or damage. Forbes, a global media outlet that focuses on business, investing and entrepreneurship, has shown how unwanted future occurring consequences can usually be traced to one of four causes: ignorance, human error, the prioritising of immediate needs over those of tomorrow, or a misalignment of values. One way to limit undesirable spillovers is to conduct a pre-mortem. Pre-mortems force policymakers and executives to imagine that their project went disastrously wrong and to generate plausible reasons why. Teams then work to build contingencies into their plans designed to eliminate potential unintended consequences. Although the approach is never failsafe, it can minimise the chances of unfortunate consequences. It can also help in mitigation should an organisation or firm be accused of unethical practices in future.

Transparency. *Are your business practices, products and procedures open and transparent?*

Practices, products and policies should be executed transparently. If this is not possible, then the advice is that they should be re-examined. Citizens and consumers alike share strong preferences for open and fair government and business procedures. So much so that, in 2023, the UK's Financial Conduct Authority – a regulator for banks, financial institutions and insurers – implemented a Consumer Duty mandate designed to set higher and clearer standards of customer protection. A significant feature of the policy concerns openness, transparency and a focus on delivering good outcomes for customers.

Influencing ethically for individuals

When it comes to individual influence, my colleague Dr Gregory Neidert, a psychologist at Arizona State University, has observed how people typically adopt one of three kinds of approach when attempting to persuade others. In the first, the *bungler* legitimately creates influence opportunities for themselves but fails to recognise or use them. Second is the *smuggler*, who seeks to exploit and serve their own needs. Third, and preferred, is the *detective*, who is able to acquire short- and longer-term influence to the benefit of all concerned. Let's take a closer look at each.

Bunglers

A few years ago my team engaged in a programme of work with a manufacturer of high-end medical diagnostic equipment: CT scanners, X-ray machines and ultrasounds. To help us understand the business, the company's managers arranged for a few of us to go out on the road and shadow their commercial and service teams who would visit hospitals, dentists and veterinary clinics to find out customer requirements and help to maintain equipment. One day in particular looms large in my memory.

It started routinely enough. Over coffee, the company representative described the various customers and sites we would be visiting over the course of the day. Despite meticulous preparation, his plan was almost immediately shelved when an important customer called him in a state of distress. The client, an experienced radiographer, explained that he was leading a training session for trainee medics later that day. Earlier in the week before leaving for a work trip he had left instructions for some spare transducers (probes) to be ordered, so that his students could practise with them. But when he arrived at his clinic that morning, he realised no one had acted on his request. Could his supplier help to save his training session and the inevitable blushes that would result?

I overheard the representative reply that he would do everything he could to help and promised to call the customer back within an hour. He then set to work. These were the days before online deliveries within hours were the norm. Besides, medical equipment like this is not available to just anyone – protocols needed to be followed. The company's main storage facility was too far away to respond quickly enough, so the representative instead called a regional office to enquire whether it had spares. Having secured a couple of transducers, he then called some of his other customers located close by to see whether he could "borrow" the remainder. Within an hour he was calling his client to report that he had secured enough probes for the training session and was now en route to deliver them. We ordered take-away coffees and set off on the two-hour drive – he feeling like a superhero and me, having witnessed his impressive efforts, feeling like a vicarious one.

The look on his customer's face when we arrived a couple of hours later, having detoured to various pick-ups on route, was a picture of relief and gratitude. "When I arrived this morning, I saw little alternative but to cancel my training clinics," he explained. "You've got me out a proper fix. Thank you, so much. I really appreciate it."

"It's really no bother at all," came the reply. "Consider it all part of the service. I'd do it for anyone."

Leaving his smiling and relieved customer, I asked the representative about the customer he had just gone to extraordinary lengths to help. "As a teaching doctor he is pretty important and quite influential," he told me. "The ultimate decision-maker, though, is his boss. He's a tough nut to crack. And he has little time for us reps. It's really hard to get an appointment with him."

I remained silent, wondering if and when the penny might drop. Few refuse a legitimate request that comes from someone who has just helped them. Particularly, as you will recall from the principle of reciprocity, if that help is delivered in the unexpected and significant way my sales friend had ably demonstrated. Of course, to respond in that moment by demanding an appointment with his boss would have seemed contrived and inappropriate, encroaching on the domain of Neidert's second type of influencer who we'll talk about next. Nevertheless, in the following days I wondered whether my friend would pick up the phone to enquire how his customer's training clinic went. And, after surely receiving another signal of heartfelt thanks, ask if he would be willing to help him arrange an appointment with his boss. I would bet good money that if he did, his grateful customer would do his absolute utmost to make sure he would get that much-prized appointment.

Sometimes the ability to persuade others successfully is a function of good timing: the boss happened to be in a good mood; last month's profits led an otherwise frugal finance manager to be uncharacteristically extravagant. But we also create moments. We provide useful information to those in need, do favours for people requiring help or offer excellent customer service to clients, as was the case of our medical imaging friend who went to great lengths to help someone in a tight spot. It is easy to respond to the resultant appreciation or thanks with a shrug of the shoulders and a "no problem". But when you do that, you potentially throw away a persuasive moment of power. To paraphrase Greg Neidert, you bungle the opportunity.

Smugglers

In contrast to the bungler, the smuggler is a different character entirely. The smuggler exploits or entirely fabricates opportunities for influence and uses them in a manipulative fashion to gain at the expense of others. Examples abound: colleagues who conceal information, or those who are selective about what they share and with whom, playing one colleague or customer off against another. And, of course, those who trade in outright falsehoods.

But not all smuggler behaviour is necessarily premeditated. In the spring of 2000 the UK found itself in a petrol crisis: supplies were being disrupted by the blockading of oil refineries by protestors. Businesses were getting desperate, schools and office attendances dropped, shops were struggling to find customers and some public services were at risk of closure. The shortage had another impact too: driver behaviour. Long queues of motorists formed outside petrol stations that were said to have supplies. As the shortage worsened the behaviour of some motorists became more extreme. News outlets reported drivers sleeping overnight in their cars, hoping to be first in line for an overnight delivery rumoured to have made it through the blockades. Others, after learning of a distant garage with supplies, would drive miles to top up with fuel despite their already three-quarters-full tank being more than ample for their immediate needs. As we have seen, scarcity, whether real or rumoured, has a potent influence on our actions, even if we ourselves have enough of what is in short supply.

News quickly spread of petrol stations that reportedly were receiving supplies, leaving lucky forecourt owners to make hay. But for one garage owner the temptation proved too much. Recognising the position he found himself in, and seeing the growing queue outside, he instructed his staff to raise pump prices. Given the context, few people would begrudge a small premium being added, but he increased his prices nearly six-fold. Although outraged, some customers still paid. Within a matter of hours he sold out, but the consequences of his actions were disastrous. Most people simply boycotted his business. Others, though, went further, making it a mission to highlight to as many as possible what an unprincipled guy he was. His business lost nearly every regular customer and his damaged reputation forced him to close soon afterwards.[7]

But perhaps the garage owner's actions are understandable. The modern-day world often places people in a dilemma where the need to make a quick, sometimes immediate, decision may not be compatible with the time needed to consider the consequences. The first thing that comes to mind might be the most efficient. It could also be the most effective and even the most lucrative. But not necessarily the most ethical.

Detectives

That's not to say that short-term success as an influencer always comes at a long-term cost. It is possible to influence people successfully in a way that builds and maintains connections and relationships so people will want to be persuaded by you today, and in the future. Neidert calls this the detective's approach.

The detective of influence takes a moment to step back to

see what components of the Influence Equation are genuinely available in a situation. What opportunities are there to frame evidence and information in a compelling way? What economic incentives could be deployed that will motivate people to engage without leaving them feeling exploited? And what emotional appeals could, when activated, satisfy an influence target's fundamental motivation to make the accurate decision, the connected decision and the decision that leaves them feeling good about themselves?

Returning to our financially (and morally) bankrupt petrol station owner, let's consider some alternative options that were available to him had he paused for the briefest of moments and taken a detective's approach to influence. He could have instructed his staff to ensure that local and regular customers were prioritised and, in doing so, make a point of informing them that he valued their custom and loyalty. He might have put up a sign publicly declaring his refusal to fleece needy motorists in their time of need: an act against his own self-interest that surely would do much to boost his reputation as a likeable and trustworthy local businessman. And rather than raising prices, staff could have asked if customers would be willing to make an additional purchase from the shop. In contrast to the actions of other businesses exploiting the situation, perhaps some of his customers would feel grateful for not being taken advantage of.

In doing so, the garage owner would also be demonstrating a set of principles that arguably provide the most helpful (and succinct) checklist when it comes to determining whether any influence strategy you deploy is likely to be an ethical influence at work. Unsurprisingly, it follows the now familiar rule of three.

1. Is my approach truthful?
2. Is it wise?
3. Does it pass the favourite sister test? (Would I be happy for someone else to use this same strategy on one of my loved ones?)

There is no doubt that the ability to influence and persuade others is an indispensable skill. This is especially true at work where influence lies at the heart of leadership, relationship building, successful negotiation, effective sales and marketing, and change. This is why influence and persuasion skills are so prized by managers and feature so highly in LinkedIn surveys. If work is about getting things done, then influence is the means to achieving it. Used effectively and ethically, influence is akin to a superpower in its ability to capture attention, win over the sceptics, sway the undecided and mobilise people to change.

But just because we can influence people doesn't mean we necessarily should always do so. At least not without some consideration of the ethical dilemmas and implications that the practice of influence invariably presents. Should we choose the unwise path, then we should also be prepared to find that it is ourselves who end up being dispensed with.

Epilogue

This is a book about how to be more influential, primarily at work, although its lessons and insights can equally be applied to influencing and persuading people in your personal life. Central to the book is the claim that anyone can be more influential at work by applying the Influence Equation. In the same way that a huge range of colours can be created by combining different quantities of the primary colours red, yellow and blue, the Influence Equation allows you to construct a large range of successful and tailored influence strategies by combining the right mix of evidence, economics and emotions appropriate to your situation.

But even a comprehensive understanding of the rules and tools of influence doesn't necessarily guarantee success, for a simple reason. Knowing is not the same as doing, which raises a crucial question that any aspiring influence master must be able to answer.

How do you know if you have influence?

$$\text{influence} = \frac{\text{evidence} + \text{economics} + \text{emotion}}{\text{context}}$$

The Influence Equation can help answer this question. First consider emotions. Your mood and emotional state ebbs and flows throughout the day, primarily in response to the variety of situations and scenarios in which you find yourself. After receiving positive feedback for a job well done you might experience a boost in confidence, a feeling that could elevate your ability to convince others. In contrast, a cutting comment or snide remark can dent confidence, which might trigger feelings of doubt and uncertainty – hardly a helpful emotional state to experience before seeking to influence others.

Consequently, just as a master influencer monitors the moods of their audience, ensuring that those people they seek to persuade are readied to receive their message, so too do they tune into their own and the impact it can have on their own effectiveness. In other words, the master influencer must be emotionally prepared and ready to persuade.

Now to economics. Modern society serves up a plentiful supply of rewards to those who have influence, and less for those who don't. To enjoy influence is to enjoy its spoils, or at least have the option to. The financial rewards are obvious, but incentives don't only come in the form of monetary gains. Non-financial rewards are also a signal of your influence: opportunities to further your skills by being selected to attend training and mentorship programmes, recognition and encouragement from those higher up, a growing professional and personal network, and all the opportunities that arise from a burgeoning set of connections. All are signals of your current (or growing) influence.

In this context influence might come across as entirely self-serving. To some degree, it is. Some people might even conclude that influence is an entirely mercenary endeavour. Again, this might be true for a minority. Others might have entirely altruistic motivations and, having gained greater influence, use it to support and improve causes bigger than themselves. Few would object to charities, aid workers and peacekeepers being afforded the resources that can improve the lives of many. For most of us, however, influence is simply a tool, albeit an important one, that helps make our journey through our professional and personal life a little easier.

Finally, evidence. It is this component of the Influence Equation that arguably provides the best indication of how influential you are. You know you have influence when you notice more people coming to you for advice and insight than vice versa. Note that this is very different to simply having followers. There is no question that the number of followers you have on social media could be seen as a yardstick of your popularity and, subsequently, your potential influence. But if your goal is to be more influential at work, to ensure that people listen to you, take you seriously and get stuff done, it's not necessary to have thousands of followers. What you need is a strategy that persuades the right people to seek you out for wisdom and advice. That's when you know you truly have influence. It may take time, but it is eminently achievable. It just requires a little forethought, preparation and planning.

A plan to get influence

The route to growing your influence is the planned and considered use of the Influence Equation. Unfortunately the pressures of modern-day life frequently limit the time and space people have available to plan properly and consider how to influence others. The cost, however, is a high likelihood of missteps and missed opportunities. A failure to plan is really a plan for failure.

So assuming you are serious about improving your influence, and you have even a modest amount of time to hatch a plan, let me end with a few pointers in the form of an Influence at Work checklist, comprising (naturally) three straightforward steps that can help.

Step 1. Target

First, consider what you want. And be specific. This might sound obvious but it's amazing how frequently people assert their influence goals in broad, even vague, ways. "I want to persuade our customers to engage with our content." "I need my team to trust each other more." "I want to convince senior management to be more supportive." "We need to influence our client base better." No doubt these are desirable goals. But they are also open to interpretation and misunderstanding. A more useful way of creating specific influence goals is to use a technique called video-talk. Video-talk works by describing your influence goal in a way that your smartphone could film it. Ask yourself: "If I pointed my phone at my desired outcome or goal, what would it see and hear?" The answer is a much more specific and well-defined influence goal that makes step 2 of the Influence at Work checklist much easier.

Step 2. Think

Now you have a specific goal, think through each component of the Influence Equation in turn and consider how it applies to your objective. Start with any evidence that supports your case. To optimise your case, what will you compare your evidence to? Who is the best messenger to deliver your message? (Being open to the fact it may not be you.) And remember the rule of three: convey your evidence using a maximum of three points or takeaways.

Next think about the economics of your case – financial and otherwise – that are available to you and consider how you could use them. Can you frame their timing and frequency to make them more attractive to the people you are persuading? Consider the pros and cons of presenting your case in terms of what people will gain, or alternatively what they stand to lose.

Remember the importance of ownership when using a loss message, and think carefully about how you will communicate your message in a way that maintains connection with your audience and avoids alienating them.

Finally, think specifically about the emotional state it would be helpful for your audience to be feeling before making your case. Is it fear, curiosity, awe, happiness, empathy – or something else? Consider too an appropriate analogy or anecdote that could serve as the vehicle for you to transport your influence appeal.

Step 3. Tailor

Having thought through these first two steps, you should now have all the ingredients to create your influence strategy. One final task remains: to consider the context and choose the appropriate combination of evidence, economics and emotion for the situation. If your audience is primarily concerned about, let's say, budgets or the cost of living, then consider prioritising the economics of your case over evidence or emotions. It will be different, however, if you are presenting to a team of lawyers or scientists who might value facts over feelings and finance. (And in the case of judges and lawyers, check they have eaten first!) And if your audience is primarily focused on how your proposal will affect people and relationships, you should prioritise the emotional component of the Influence Equation over economics and evidence.

Ultimately, how you use the Influence Equation will be a combination of its three nominators (evidence, economics and emotions), the context you are operating in and, importantly, your personal style. The Influence Equation is not designed to offer a standardised approach to persuading others. In fact, the exact opposite is true. I present it as a way of thinking that allows you to tailor a variety of influence strategies and tactics to address the many and various situations you will face throughout your working life. And to do so in a way that doesn't compromise who you are, your values or your integrity.

This is important because, ultimately, influence that works is a human affair.

Acknowledgements

I can't be the only author who doesn't find the book-writing process, replete with its looming deadlines, periods of self-doubt and hours spent willing words to appear as if by magic on a barren screen, to be an especially uplifting experience. (Although that does change a bit once the work is done.) Luckily, they are challenges I have previously been able to share, given my good fortune to co-author with Robert Cialdini, Noah Goldstein and Joe Marks on prior works. To this day I remain convinced it is their insights, smarts and reputations that contribute far more to the continuing success of our books than anything of my own doing. I will be forever grateful to each of them.

Consequently, I had no plans to repeat the process, solo.

But one day I received an unexpected call from Clare Grist Taylor, my editor at Profile Books, informing me of a new series of works she was curating for *The Economist* and gauging my interest in participating. The draw of working with Clare again, as well as writing for a newspaper and publisher whose work and reputation I have long admired, was a strong one. Besides, Clare is someone it is hard to say no to (and as a result probably has little need for a book like this). So, I begin these acknowledgments with my appreciation to Clare for not only inviting me to write for her again, but also for being a guiding light and source of support throughout. I also extend thanks to Paul Forty, Georgia Poplett, Philippa Logan and Andrew

Franklin at Profile Books and to Zanny Minton Beddoes, Tom Standage, Martin Adams, Stephen Somerville, Siriliya Nawalkar and Fionnuala Duggan at *The Economist*.

The incredible team at Influence at Work also deserve my deep gratitude. Sophie Armour, Eloise Copland, David Crichton-Miller, Andrea Fines-Allin, Clara Federrath, Bobette Gorden, Dr Amanda Henwood, Dr Nick Hobson, Dr Greg Neidert, Araminta Naylor, Nina Norris, Dr Keith O'Brien, Olivia Pattison, Owen Powell, Sebastian Roca, Alex Rusby, Catherine Scott, Julian Seaward, Eily VanderMeer and Audrey Van Rueckmann are a joy to work with and who collectively contribute to a working environment that every day offers up an invigorating mix of purpose, pleasure, challenge and new discovery. They serve our clients brilliantly and represent the very best that the world of applied behavioural science has to offer. Special thanks go to Audrey von Rueckmann for her valuable assistance fact-checking and referencing. To Nick Hobson who helped my thinking in structuring chapters and for his expertise on the psychology of emotions. And especially to Olivia Pattison who not only helped in the book's early stages, but also graciously permitted me to adapt some of her original research on ethics.

For more than two decades I have been the lucky recipient of advice, insights, support and opportunities from a wonderful array of people who I have been inspired by, learned from, made friends with, partnered and worked with at Influence at Work. Invariably I will have omitted a few names and seek their understanding that this is entirely unintentional and something I will endeavour to address on future print runs. They are Wing Ah, Alex Aiken, Mike Aldrich, Adam Alter, Keith Anderson, Debbie Androlia, Vicky Ashworth, Brendan Barns, Senator John Barrasso, Nick Barron, Suraj Bassi, Tim Batchelor, Matt Battersby, Karen Beattie, Scott Berinato,

Richard Bevan OBE, Alex Bigg, Octavius Black, Rob Blackie, Bastien Blain, Vanessa Bohns, Chris Brady, Anita Braga, Brian Brennan, Nicole Brigandi, John Bunch, Ian Burbridge, Patrick Campal-Lindahl, Eoin Cannon, Dame Louise Casey, Malik Chalid, Chris Chapman, Alex Chesterfield, Margi Clarke, Daniel Crewe, Bruce Daisley, Marco Del Mancino, Rebecca Dell, Paul Dolan, Cheryl Donnelly, Kirstie Donnelly, Nick Down, Peter Duffy, Rupert Dunbar-Rees, Adam Edwards, Shane Ellison, Torben Emmerling, Antoine Ferrere, Lord (Danny) Finkelstein, Becky Gentle, Steven Gerrard, Dimitrios Georgiopoulos, Dan Gertsacov, Rob Gibby, Keith Gladdis, Noah Goldstein, Ali Goldsworthy, Kate Gomes, Karen Gonsalkorale, Lauren Gordon, Adam Grant, Deborah Green, Vlad Griskevicius, Alex Guariento, David Halpern, Heather Hancock, Alison Hankey, Akira Haraguchi, Sharon Hardcastle, Tim Harford, Verne Harnish, Will Heald, Andy Hedge, Fred Hockenjos, Tim Hulse, Daniel Kahneman (RIP), Guy Kawasaki, Louise Keen, Alex Khaldi, Ipsitaa Khullar, Ruth Killick, Adam Kingl, Hilary Kitson, Jurgen Klopp, Michelle Klotz, Martin Knight, Anna Koczwara, John Lambert, Julie Lardelli, Kathy Large, Betty Lau, Rachel Le Sueur, Yann Leriche, Jim Levine, Professor Eric Levy, Dan Listemann, Anthony Madonna, Thierry Mallet, Helen Mankin, Daniel Marcos, Costas Markides, Joe Marks, Jonathan Marshall, Karthi Martelli, Alan McDougall, Sue McKellar, Paul McKenna, Bob McKenzie, John Phillip Martin, Hannah McQuoid-Mason, Stephan Meier, Rob Metcalfe, Andrew Middleton, John 'Mitch' Mitchell, Annie Montmarquette, Lee Morley, Ellie Mulholland, Neil Mullarkey, Oded Netzer, James Nicholls, Mike Norton, Jeff Nott, Olivier Oullier, Rebecca Parcolazo-Rudge, Ed Percival (RIP), Bennedetta Peto, Nick Pope, Maddie Quinlan, Alan Ramsay, Karen Reffitt, Kim Royds, Amy Scorgie, Doug Scott, Meera Shah, Dil Sidhu, Alan Snow, Alice Soriano, Jim Souter,

Emma Sterland, Nigel Stephens, Margaret Stockham, Matthew Stork, Cass Sunstein, Timea Tarczy, Matthew Taylor, Sarah Tobitt (RIP), Cara Tracy, Dimitrios Tsivikos, Chiara Varazzani, Marielle Villamaux, Ivo Vlaev, Nuala Walsh, Tony Ware (NP will understand), Ania Wieckowski, Nigel Wilcockson, Rick Wolff, Sue Yip and Todd Zavodnick.

Finally, to Lindsay Martin and Robert Cialdini. Of all the people I have been fortunate to have encountered, you two stand out, personally and professionally. I dedicate this to you both.

Notes

Chapter 2: The history of influence

1. A. Roccati, "Dating Ptahhotep's maxims (Note Letterarie VI)", *Orientalia*, 83(2) (2014), pp. 238–40.
2. V.H. Mair and L. Tzu, *Tao Te Ching: The Classic Book of Integrity and the Way* (Bantam, 2012).
3. E.M. Cope and J.E. Sandys (eds), *Aristotle: Rhetoric*, Vol. 2 (Cambridge University Press, 2010).
4. S. Danziger, J. Levav and L. Avnaim-Pesso, "Extraneous factors in judicial decisions", *Proceedings of the National Academy of Sciences*, 108(17) (2011), pp. 6889–92.
5. R. Dunkle, "Overview of Roman Spectacle" in P. Christesen and D.G. Kyle (eds) *A Companion to Sport and Spectacle in Greek and Roman Antiquity* (Wiley, 2013), pp. 377–94.
6. W. Shakespeare, *All's Well That Ends Well* (Routledge, 2019).
7. O. Wilde, *The Picture of Dorian Gray* (Oxford University Press, 2006).
8. K. Lewin, "Frontiers in group dynamics: concept, method and reality in social science; social equilibria and social change", *Human Relations*, 1(1) (1947), pp. 5–41.
9. L. Festinger, *A Theory of Cognitive Dissonance* (Evanston, IL: Row, Peterson, 1957).
10. B.F. Skinner, "Operant behavior", *American Psychologist*, 18(8) (1963), pp. 503–15.
11. S.E. Asch, "Studies of independence and conformity: I. A minority of one against a unanimous majority",

Psychological Monographs: General and Applied, 70(9) (1956), pp. 1–70.

12. M. Sherif et al., *Intergroup Conflict and Cooperation: The Robbers Cave Experiment* (University Book Exchange, 1961).

13. C. Rogers, *Client-Centered Therapy* (Hachette, 2012).

14. D. Carnegie, *How to Win Friends and Influence People* (Simon & Schuster, 1936).

15. R.B. Cialdini, *Influence: The Psychology of Persuasion* (HarperCollins, 2021).

Chapter 3: Influence: meanings, myths and motivations

1. N. Machiavelli, *The Prince* (1513) (Hertfordshire: Wordsworth Editions, 1993).

2. J.J. Skowronski and D.E Carlston, "Negativity and extremity biases in impression formation: a review of explanations", *Psychological Bulletin*, 105(1) (1989), p. 131.

3. S. Martin and J. Marks, *Messengers: Who We Listen To, Who We Don't, and Why* (Random House, 2019).

4. J. Zenger and J. Folkman, "Feedback: the powerful paradox", White paper, Zenger Folkman (2015).

5. D. Ramsey, "UC San Diego experts calculate how much information Americans consume", physorg.com (December 14th 2009).

6. S. Kemp, "Digital 2021: Global Overview Report", datareportal.com (January 27th 2021). datareportal.com/reports/digital-2021-global-overview-report

7. R.R. Briefel and C.L. Johnson, "Secular trends in dietary intake in the United States", *Annual Review of Nutrition*, 24 (2004), pp. 401–31.

8. Pangolin facts, WWF. www.worldwildlife.org/species/pangolin

9. "Illegal wildlife trade crisis", Zoological Society of London.

10. Influence at Work (2021). Data on file.

11. A.A. Long, *Epictetus: A Stoic and Socratic Guide to Life* (Oxford University Press, 2002).
12. P.W. Schultz et al., "The constructive, destructive, and reconstructive power of social norms", *Psychological Science*, 18(5) (2007), pp. 429–34.
13. Hansard, "Businesses: Small and Medium-Sized Enterprises", Vol. 753 (May 6th 2014). hansard.parliament. uk/Lords/2014-05-06/debates/14050619000597/ BusinessesSmallAndMedium-SizedEnterprises#contribut ion-14050619000291
14. H.A. Simon, *Models of Bounded Rationality: Empirically Grounded Economic Reason*, Vol. 3 (MIT Press, 1997).
15. J.B. Harvey, "The Abilene paradox: the management of agreement", *Organisational Dynamics*, 3(1) (1974), pp. 63–80.
16. I.L. Janis, "Groupthink", *IEEE Engineering Management Review*, 36(1) (2008), p. 36.
17. M.D. Alicke and O. Govorun, "The better-than-average effect" in M.D. Alicke, D.A. Dunning and J.I. Krueger (eds), *The Self in Social Judgment* (Psychology Press, 2005), pp. 85–106.
18. A.M. Grant and D.A. Hofmann, "It's not all about me: motivating hand hygiene among health care professionals by focusing on patients", *Psychological Science*, 22(12) (2011), pp. 1494–9.

Chapter 4: Influencing with evidence

1. W.E. Deming, *The New Economics for Industry, Education, Government* (MIT Press, 1994).
2. D.A. Garvin, *Managing Quality: The Strategic and Competitive Edge* (Simon & Schuster, 1988).
3. M.P. Jiménez-Aleixandre and S. Erduran, "Argumentation in science education: an overview" in S. Erduran and

   M.P. Jiménez-Aleixandre (eds), *Argumentation in Science Education: Perspectives from Classroom-Based Research* (Springer, 2007), pp. 3–27.
4. E. Ogbonna and L.C. Harris, "Leadership style, organisational culture and performance: empirical evidence from UK companies", *International Journal of Human Resource Management*, 11(4) (2000), pp. 766–88.
5. J.K. Aronson, "Anecdotes as evidence", *BMJ*, 326(7403) (2003) p. 1346.
6. D. Kahneman, J.L. Knetsch and R.H. Thaler, "Anomalies: the endowment effect, loss aversion, and status quo bias", *Journal of Economic Perspectives*, 5(1) (1991), pp. 193–206.
7. S.M. Smith and R.E. Petty, "Message framing and persuasion: a message processing analysis", *Personality and Social Psychology Bulletin*, 22(3) (1996), pp. 257–68.
8. N.H. Anderson and A.A. Barrios, "Primacy effects in personality impression formation", *Journal of Abnormal and Social Psychology*, 63(2) (1961), pp. 346–50.
9. Influence at Work (2012). Data on file.
10. N.P. Miller (ed.), *Tacitus: Annals XV* (Bristol Classical Press, 1994).
11. S. Martin and J. Marks, *Messengers: Who We Listen To, Who We Don't, and Why* (Random House, 2019).
12. Influence at Work (2008). Data on file.
13. F. J. Flynn, "How much should I give and how often? The effects of generosity and frequency of favor exchange on social status and productivity", *Academy of Management Journal*, 46(5) (2003), pp. 539–53.
14. B.F.S. Southard and B.A.S. Southard, "Edward Everett, 'Gettysburg Address' (19 November 1863)", "Abraham Lincoln, 'Gettysburg Address' (19 November 1863)", (2009).
15. A. Lincoln, *The Gettysburg Address* (Penguin, 2009).

16. D.C. Feiler, L.P. Tost and A.M. Grant, "Mixed reasons, missed givings: the costs of blending egoistic and altruistic reasons in donation requests", *Journal of Experimental Social Psychology*, 48(6) (2012), pp. 1322–8.
17. S.B. Shu and K.A. Carlson, "When three charms but four alarms: identifying the optimal number of claims in persuasion settings", *Journal of Marketing*, 78(1) (2014), pp. 127–39.

Chapter 5: Influencing with economics

1. E. Fehr and A. Falk, "Psychological foundations of incentives", *European Economic Review*, 46(4–5) (2002), pp. 687–724.
2. M. Mackerras and I. McAllister, "Compulsory voting, party stability and electoral advantage in Australia", *Electoral Studies*, 18(2) (1999), pp. 217–33.
3. K.N. Kirby, "Bidding on the future: evidence against normative discounting of delayed rewards", *Journal of Experimental Psychology: General*, 126(1) (1997), pp. 54–70.
4. I. Mathauer and I. Imhoff, "Health worker motivation in Africa: the role of non-financial incentives and human resource management tools", *Human Resources for Health*, 4(24) (2006), pp. 1–17.
5. L.J. Bellamy, "Exploring the relationship between major hazard, fatal and non-fatal accidents through outcomes and causes", *Safety Science*, 71(B) (2015), pp. 93–103.
6. M.T. Wolf and J.W. Burdick, "Artificial potential functions for highway driving with collision avoidance", in *IEEE International Conference on Robotics and Automation* (IEEE, 2008), pp. 3731–6.
7. Influence at Work (2018). Data on file.
8. Ibid.

9. U. Gneezy, S. Meier and P. Rey-Biel, "When and why incentives (don't) work to modify behavior", *Journal of Economic Perspectives*, 25(4) (2011), pp. 191–210.

10. C.K. Hsee et al., Unit asking: a method to boost donations and beyond", *Psychological Science*, 24(9) (2013), pp. 1801–8.

11. R.H. Thaler, "Mental accounting matters", *Journal of Behavioral Decision Making*, 12(3), (1999), pp. 183–206.

12. R.L. Soster, A.D. Gershoff and W.O. Bearden, "The bottom dollar effect: the influence of spending to zero on pain of payment and satisfaction", *Journal of Consumer Research*, 41(3) (2014), pp. 656–77.

13. H. Bembenutty, "Sustaining motivation and academic goals: the role of academic delay of gratification", *Learning and Individual Differences*, 11(3) (1999), pp. 233–57.

14. N. Novemsky and D. Kahneman, "The boundaries of loss aversion", *Journal of Marketing Research*, 42(2) (2005), pp. 119–28.

15. E.R. Frederiks, K. Stenner and E.V. Hobman, "Household energy use: applying behavioural economics to understand consumer decision-making and behaviour", *Renewable and Sustainable Energy Reviews*, 41(Jan) (2015), pp. 1385–94.

16. D. Kahneman, "Prospect theory: an analysis of decision under risk", *Econometrica*, 47(2) (1979), p. 278.

17. A.J. Rothman et al., "The influence of message framing on intentions to perform health behaviors", *Journal of Experimental Social Psychology*, 29(5) (1993), pp. 408–33.

18. H. Leventhal, R. Singer and S. Jones, "Effects of fear and specificity of recommendation upon attitudes and behaviour", *Journal of Personality and Social Psychology*, 2(1) (1965), pp. 20–29.

19. T. Hossain and J.A. List, "The behavioralist visits the factory: increasing productivity using simple framing

manipulations", *Management Science*, 58(12) (2012),
pp. 2151–67.

20. Ibid.

21. D. Kahneman, J.L. Knetsch and R.H. Thaler, "Anomalies:
the endowment effect, loss aversion, and status quo bias",
Journal of Economic Perspectives, 5(1) (1991), pp. 193–206.

22. M.I. Norton, D. Mochon and D. Ariely, "The 'IKEA effect':
when labor leads to love", *Journal of Consumer Psychology*,
22(3) (2012), pp. 453–60.

23. P. Dolan and R. Metcalfe, "Measuring subjective wellbeing:
recommendations on measures for use by national
governments", *Journal of Social Policy*, 41(2) (2012),
pp. 409–27.

24. R. Katz and T.J. Allen, "Investigating the Not Invented Here
(NIH) syndrome: a look at the performance, tenure, and
communication patterns of 50 R&D Project Groups", *R&D
Management*, 12(1) (1982), pp. 7–20.

25. B. Flyvbjerg and D. Gardner, *How Big Things Get Done: The
Surprising Factors that Determine the Fate of Every Project,
from Home Renovations to Space Exploration and Everything
in Between* (Signal, 2023).

26. B. Flyvbjerg, "What you should know about megaprojects
and why: an overview", *Project Management Journal*,
45(2) (2014), pp. 6–19.

27. G. Castignani et al., "Driver behavior profiling using
smartphones: a low-cost platform for driver monitoring",
IEEE Intelligent Transportation Systems Magazine,
7(1) (2015), pp. 91–102.

Chapter 6: Influencing with emotion

1. H. Damasio et al., "The return of Phineas Gage: clues about
the brain from the skull of a famous patient", *Science*,
264(5162) (1994), pp. 1102–5.

2. P.J. Schoemaker, "The expected utility model: its variants, purposes, evidence and limitations", *Journal of Economic Literature* 20(2) (1982), pp. 529–63.

3. N. Schwarz and G.L. Clore, "Feelings and phenomenal experiences", in E.T. Higgins and A.W. Kruglanski (eds), *Social Psychology: Handbook of Basic Principles* (Guildford Press, 1996), pp. 433–65.

4. A. Bechara and A.R. Damasio, "The somatic marker hypothesis: a neural theory of economic decision", *Games and Economic Behavior*, 52(2) (2005), pp. 336–72.

5. V. Griskevicius et al., "Fear and loving in Las Vegas: evolution, emotion and persuasion", *Journal of Marketing Research*, 46(3) (2009), pp. 384–95.

6. J.A. Russell, A. Weiss and G.A. Mendelsohn, "Affect grid: a single-item scale of pleasure and arousal", *Journal of Personality and Social Psychology*, 57(3) (1989), pp. 493–502.

7. J.S. Lerner, D.A. Small and G. Loewenstein, "Heart strings and purse strings: carryover effects of emotions on economic decisions", *Psychological Science*, 15(5) (2004), pp. 337–41.

8. D.T. Wegener, R.E. Petty and S.M. Smith, "Positive mood can increase or decrease message scrutiny: the hedonic contingency view of mood and message processing", *Journal of Personality and Social Psychology*, 69(1) (1995), p. 5.

9. J.S. Lerner and L.Z. Tiedens, "Portrait of the angry decision maker: how appraisal tendencies shape anger's influence on cognition", *Journal of Behavioral Decision Making*, 19(2) (2006), pp. 115–37.

10. B. Scott et al., "Health in our hands, but not in our heads: understanding hygiene motivation in Ghana", *Health Policy and Planning*, 22(4) (2007), pp. 225–33.

11. J. Haidt, (2003). "The moral emotions", in R.J. Davidson, K.R. Scherer and H.H. Goldsmith (eds), *Handbook of Affective Sciences* (*Oxford University Press*, 2003), pp. 852–70.
12. Influence at Work (2016, 2017, 2018). Data on file.
13. N. Ambady et al., "Surgeons' tone of voice: a clue to malpractice history", *Surgery*, 132(1) (2002), pp. 5–9.
14. B. Lotto and Cirque du Soleil, "How we experience awe, and why it matters", TED Talk (April 2019).
15. P.K. Piff et al., "Awe, the small self, and prosocial behavior", *Journal of Personality and Social Psychology*, 108(6) (2015), p. 883.
16. V. Bohns, *You Have More Influence Than You Think: How We Underestimate Our Powers of Persuasion, and Why It Matters* (WW Norton, 2021).
17. M.M. Roghanizad and V.K. Bohns, "Ask in person: you're less persuasive than you think over email", *Journal of Experimental Social Psychology*, 69 (2017), pp. 223–6.
18. L. Nayak et al., "A picture is worth a thousand words: needs assessment for multimedia radiology reports in a large tertiary care medical center", *Academic Radiology*, 20 (2013), pp. 1577–83.
19. "Missing person posters redesigned for more impact and will no longer have word 'missing'", SkyNews (May 25th 2022).
20. D. Gentner and A.B. Markman, "Structure mapping in analogy and similarity", *American Psychologist*, 52(1) (1997), p. 45.

Chapter 7: The principles of influence

1. R.B. Cialdini, *Influence: The Psychology of Persuasion* (HarperCollins, 2021).

2. Influence at Work, "Persuasion pilots: using the science of persuasion to drive sales results", www.influenceatwork. com/wp-content/uploads/2020/03/Persuasion-Pilots-McDonalds-Arcos-Dorados-INFLUENCE-AT-WORKpdf.pdf

3. N.J. Goldstein, V. Griskevicius and R.B. Cialdini, "Reciprocity by proxy: a novel influence strategy for stimulating cooperation", *Administrative Science Quarterly*, 56(3) (2011), pp. 441–73.

4. Ibid.

5. D.B. Strohmetz et al., "Sweetening the till: the use of candy to increase restaurant tipping", *Journal of Applied Social Psychology*, 32(2) (2002), pp. 300–9.

6. R. Garner, "Post-it® note persuasion: a sticky influence", *Journal of Consumer Psychology*, 15(3) (2005), pp. 230–7.

7. R. Cialdini, *Pre-Suasion: A Revolutionary Way to Influence and Persuade* (Simon & Schuster, 2016).

8. D.A. Dillman, *Mail and Internet Surveys: The Tailored Design Method*, 2007 update (John Wiley, 2011).

9. M. Morris et al., "Schmooze or lose: social friction and lubrication in e-mail negotiations", *Group Dynamics: Theory, Research and Practice*, 6(1) (2002), pp. 89–100.

10. N. Grant, L.R. Fabrigar and H. Lim, "Exploring the efficacy of compliments as a tactic for securing compliance", *Basic and Applied Social Psychology*, 32(3) (2010), pp. 226–33.

11. E. Chan and J. Sengupta, "Insincere flattery actually works: a dual attitudes perspective", *Journal of Marketing Research*, 47(1) (2010), pp. 122–33.

12. M. Levine et al., "Identity and emergency intervention: how social group membership and inclusiveness of group boundaries shape helping behavior", *Personality and Social Psychology Bulletin*, 31(4) (2005), pp. 443–53.

13. J. Marks, E. Copland et al., "Epistemic spillovers: learning others' political views reduces the ability to assess and

use their expertise in nonpolitical domains", *Cognition*, 188 (2019), pp. 74–84.

14. A.N. Doob and A.E. Gross, "Status of frustrator as an inhibitor of horn-honking responses", *Journal of Social Psychology*, 76(2) (1968), pp. 213–18.

15. M. Lefkowitz, R.R. Blake and J.S. Mouton, "Status factors in pedestrian violation of traffic signals", *Journal of Abnormal and Social Psychology*, 51(3) (1955), pp. 704–6.

16. G. Castledine, "Nursing's image: it is how you use your stethoscope that counts!", *British Journal of Nursing*, 5(14), (2014), p. 882.

17. R.B. Cialdini, "The science of persuasion", *Scientific American*, 284(2) (2001), pp. 76–81.

18. F. de La Rochefoucauld, *Oeuvres complètes de La Rochefoucauld*, Vol. 1 (Garnier, 1883).

19. Influence at Work (2109). Data on file.

20. F.M. Stok et al., "Don't tell me what I should do, but what others do: the influence of descriptive and injunctive peer norms on fruit consumption in adolescents", *British Journal of Health Psychology*, 19(1) (2014), pp. 52–64.

21. J.M. Nolan, J. Kenefick and P.W. Schultz, "Normative messages promoting energy conservation will be underestimated by experts ... unless you show them the data", *Social Influence*, 6(3) (2011), pp. 169–80.

22. S. Martin, "98% of HBR readers love this article", *Harvard Business Review*, 90 (2012), pp. 23–25.

23. Influence at Work (2109). Data on file.

24. "Applying behavioural insights to organ donation", Report, Behavioural Insights Team (2013).

25. S.J. Martin, S. Bassi and R. Dunbar-Rees, "Commitments, norms and custard creams: a social influence approach to reducing did not attends (DNAs)", *Journal of the Royal Society of Medicine*, 105(3) (2012), pp. 101–4.

26. Ibid.
27. W. Abrahamse et al., "A review of intervention studies aimed at household energy conservation", *Journal of Environmental Psychology*, 25(3) (2005), pp. 273–91.
28. A. Knishinsky, "The effects of scarcity of material and exclusivity of information on industrial buyer perceived risk in provoking a purchase decision", unpublished doctoral dissertation (Arizona State University, 1982).

Chapter 8: The practice of influence

1. *How You Really Make Decisions*, BBC 2, Horizon series (2013–14).
2. M.F. Mason et al., "Precise offers are potent anchors: conciliatory counteroffers and attributions of knowledge in negotiations", *Journal of Experimental Social Psychology*, 49(4) (2013), pp. 759–63.
3. G. Brown and M. Baer, "Location in negotiation: is there a home field advantage?", *Organisational Behavior and Human Decision Processes*, 114(2) (2011), pp. 190–200.
4. A. Koester, "Why face-to-face communication matters: a comparison of face-to-face and computer-mediated communication", in *COVID-19, Communication and Culture* (Routledge, 2022), pp. 115–34.
5. M. Lynn, "Mega tips 2: twenty tested techniques to increase your tips", eCommons, Cornell University Library (2011).
6. M. Koo and A. Fishbach, "The small-area hypothesis: effects of progress monitoring on goal adherence", *Journal of Consumer Research*, 39(3) (2012), pp. 493–509.
7. E.F. Loftus and J.C. Palmer, "Reconstruction of automobile destruction: an example of the interaction between language and memory", *Journal of Verbal Learning and Verbal Behavior*, 13(5) (1974), pp. 585–9.

8. C.J. Bryan et al., "Motivating voter turnout by invoking the self", *Proceedings of the National Academy of Sciences*, 108(31), (2011), pp. 12653–6.
9. W. Wosinska et al. (eds), *The Practice of Social Influence in Multiple Cultures* (Psychology Press, 2000).
10. D. Kahneman et al., "When more pain is preferred to less: adding a better end", *Psychological Science*, 4(6) (1993), pp. 401–5.

Chapter 9: Influencing (ethically) at work

1. K. Korosec, "Volkswagen's US auto sales got crushed in November", Fortune.com (December 1st 2015).
2. J.M. Karpoff, J.R. Lott and E.W. Wehrly, "The reputational penalties for environmental violations: empirical evidence", *Journal of Law and Economics*, 68 (2005), pp. 653–75.
3. "Growing beyond: a place for integrity", 12th Global Fraud Survey, Ernst & Young (2012).
4. C. Clavien, "Ethics of nudges: a general framework with a focus on shared preference justifications", *Journal of Moral Education*, 47(3) (2018), pp. 1–17.
5. O. Pattison, "An ethical framework", unpublished dissertation (University of Bath, 2020).
6. R.H. Thaler and C.R. Sunstein, *Nudge: The Final Edition* (Yale University Press, 2021).
7. "Fuel price protests", BBC News (May 22nd 2008). news. bbc.co.uk/2/hi/in_depth/world/2000/world_fuel_crisis/ default.stm

Index